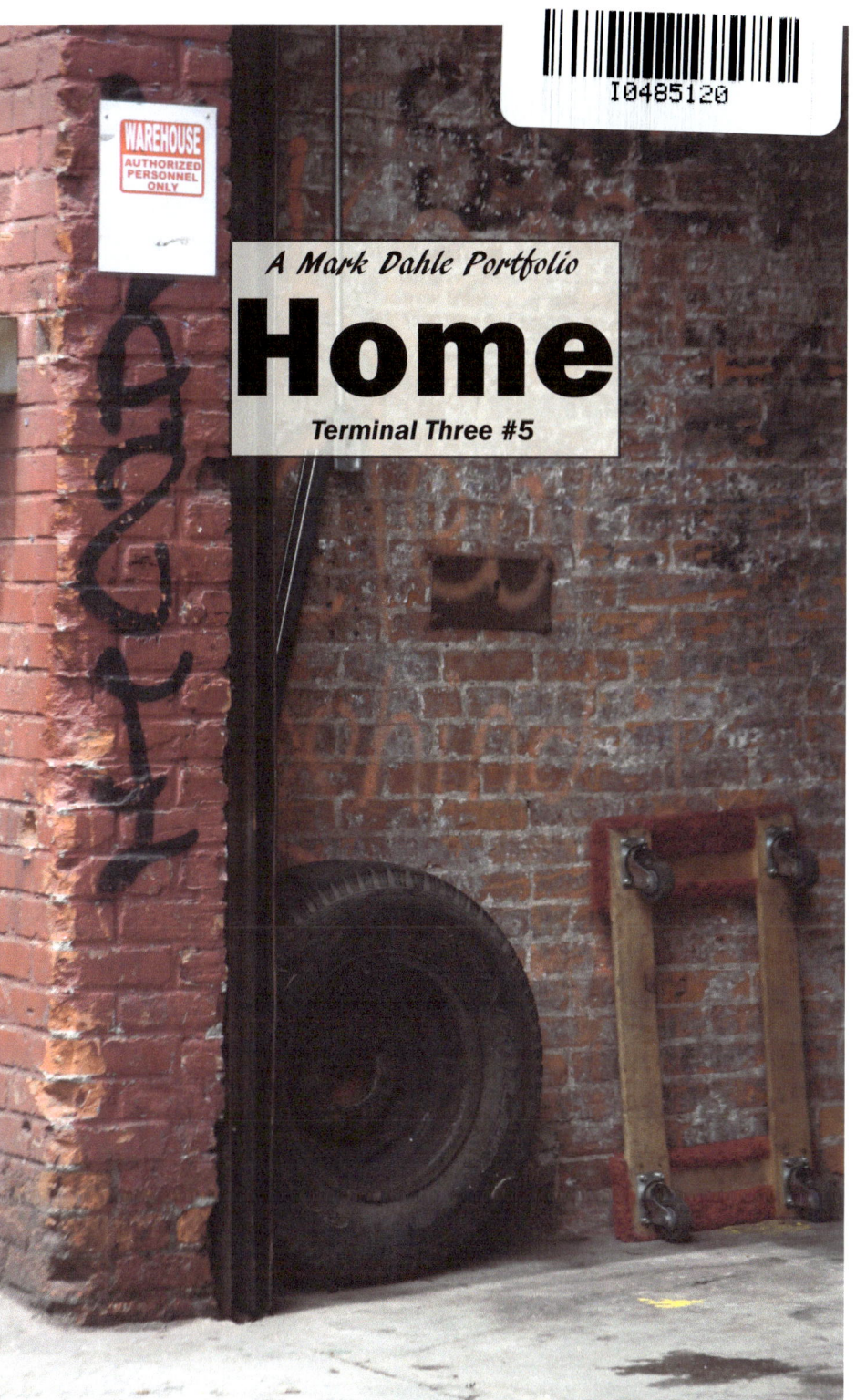

WAREHOUSE
AUTHORIZED
PERSONNEL
ONLY

A Mark Dahle Portfolio

Home

Terminal Three #5

I0485120

Mark Dahle Portfolios can be read in a few minutes and enjoyed for a lifetime.

Unlike many picture books, the text is not related to the beautiful painting at the right and the photographs that follow. This might seem a little weird at first. One thing that helps is to order more portfolios until you get used to it. In the meantime, feel free to draw your own pictures of the last day of the Otto convention if you like.

This portfolio includes a photo of a brilliant 36 x 24 inch painting (at the right), twenty-six beautiful pictures of Manhattan, and a story about the last day of the Otto convention.

Photographs in this book are available in very limited editions. See http://www.MarkDahle.com for more information and for previews of upcoming portfolios.

© Mark Dahle 2016. All rights reserved.

We do our best to create portfolios free of editing mistakes. But it's hard to catch everything. We reward people who report errors in any Mark Dahle portfolio. For details see MarkDahle.com/Typos.html or email MarkDahle@aol.com with the subject line "Typos." Thanks!

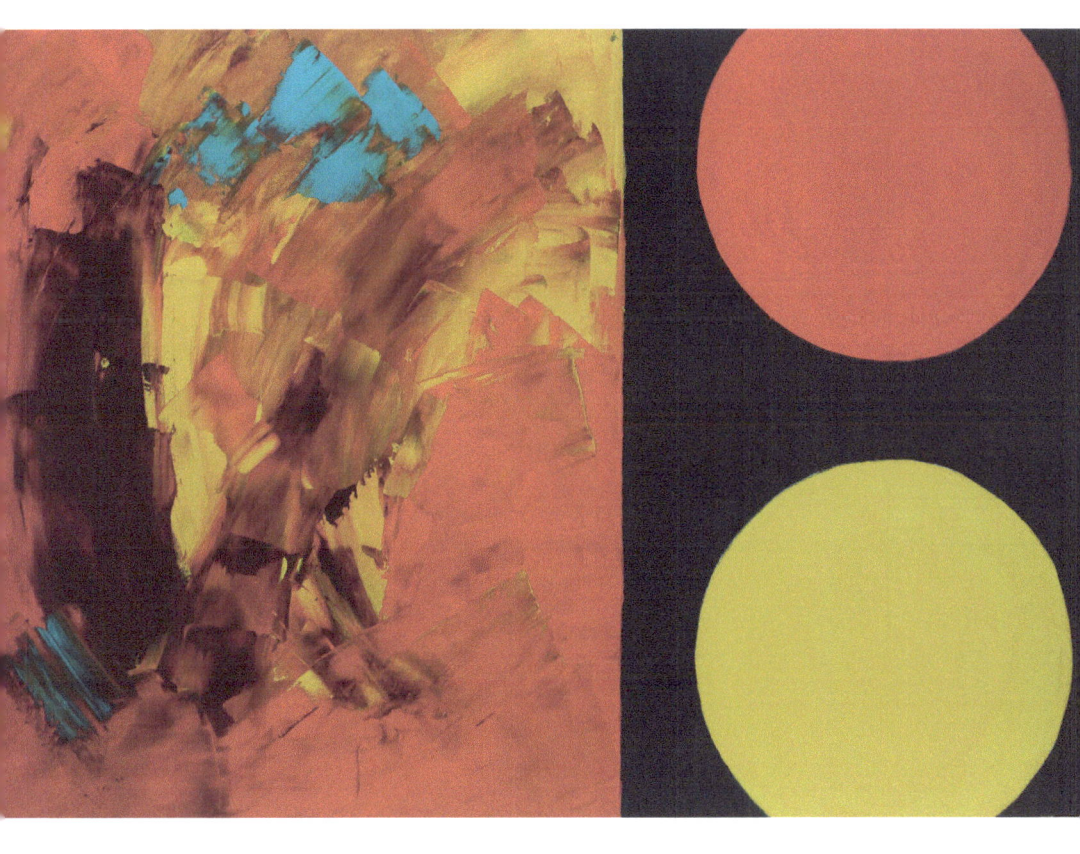

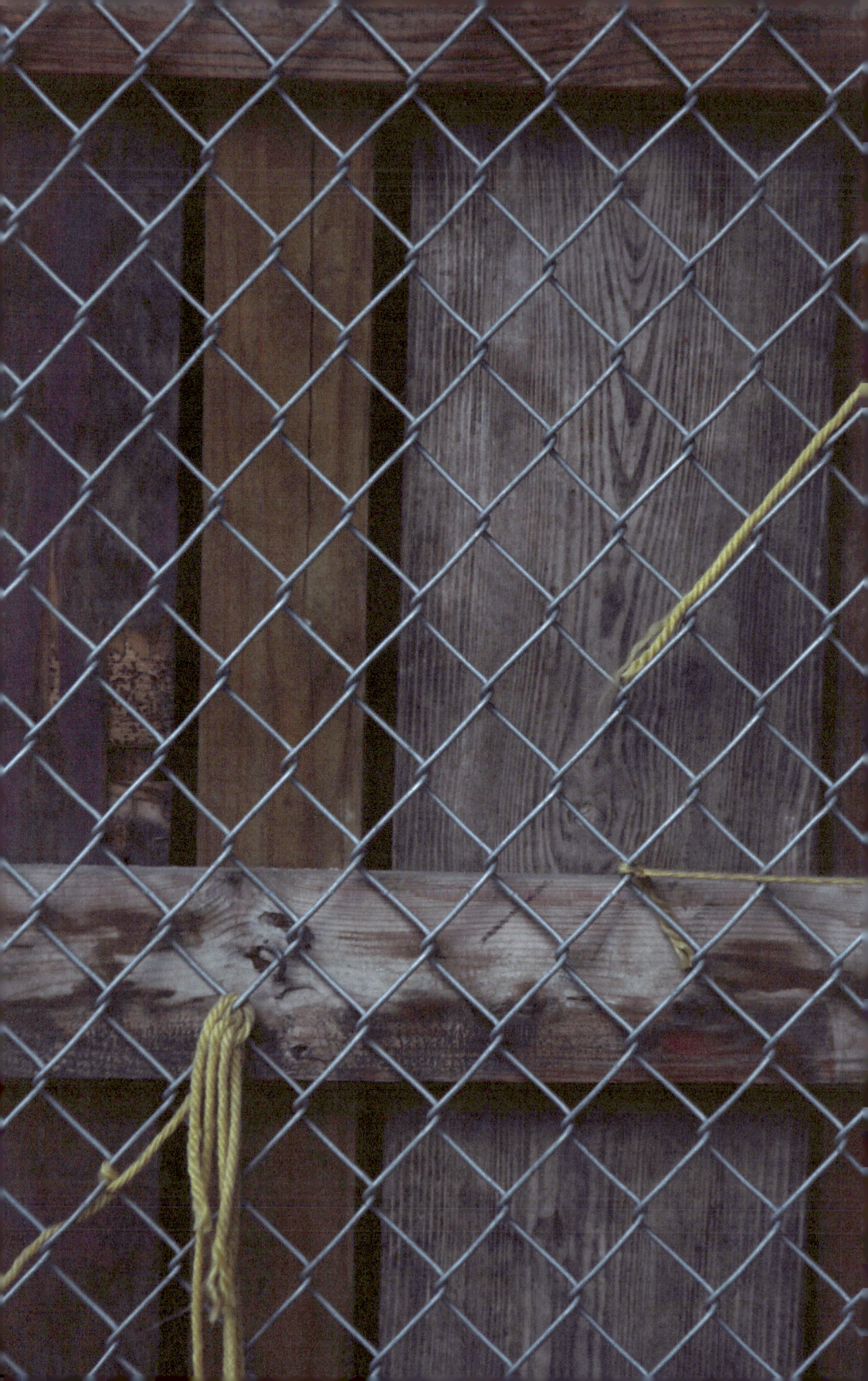

The delegates were filing into the main banquet hall for the closing ceremony. Monitors showed the activity from every angle, and even from a distance the cameras easily captured the delegates' enthusiasm.

A day before, they had been tired, cranky, and weary – exhausted after ten tumultuous days of shocks and compromises. When the convention for the Otto Party had been planned, everyone had expected three normal days of politicking with plenty of time for recreation blended in. The delegates had packed for such. But during the lockdown, with a media blackout in place, delegates had no way to call home to explain the emergencies they were facing.

Now, with the end of the convention finally in sight, delegates were excited and eager to get home. The media embargo had ended after the new President's address to the nation. That by itself relieved much of the tension the delegates had been feeling as they were finally able to place and receive calls.

This morning they had been assembled in the main auditorium so a complete roll call could be conducted. No delegate had been allowed to miss the final vote. That done, they were being shepherded in two lines into the banquet hall, getting vaccinated against MalPox on their way. As soon as everyone was through the process, they would have a celebratory lunch followed by a five-minute speech from the new President. Everyone would be starting for home within the hour.

"Package for you, Tevor."

Rick was standing near the SecurGate, holding the package up so Tevor could see it as he arrived for his shift.

"For me? From whom?"

"It doesn't say. But it requires a signature."

Tevor placed his hand on the ReceiptConfirm, then took the package. He thought about keeping it unopened in his locker until his shift was over, but he knew he would be wondering about it while working. Besides, Teri hadn't yet arrived, and they had to go through the SecurGate together.

Even though it was the first day that mail had been allowed, Tevor couldn't imagine who would send him something here. At home, yes. But at ConventionControl? Why not send a VidText?

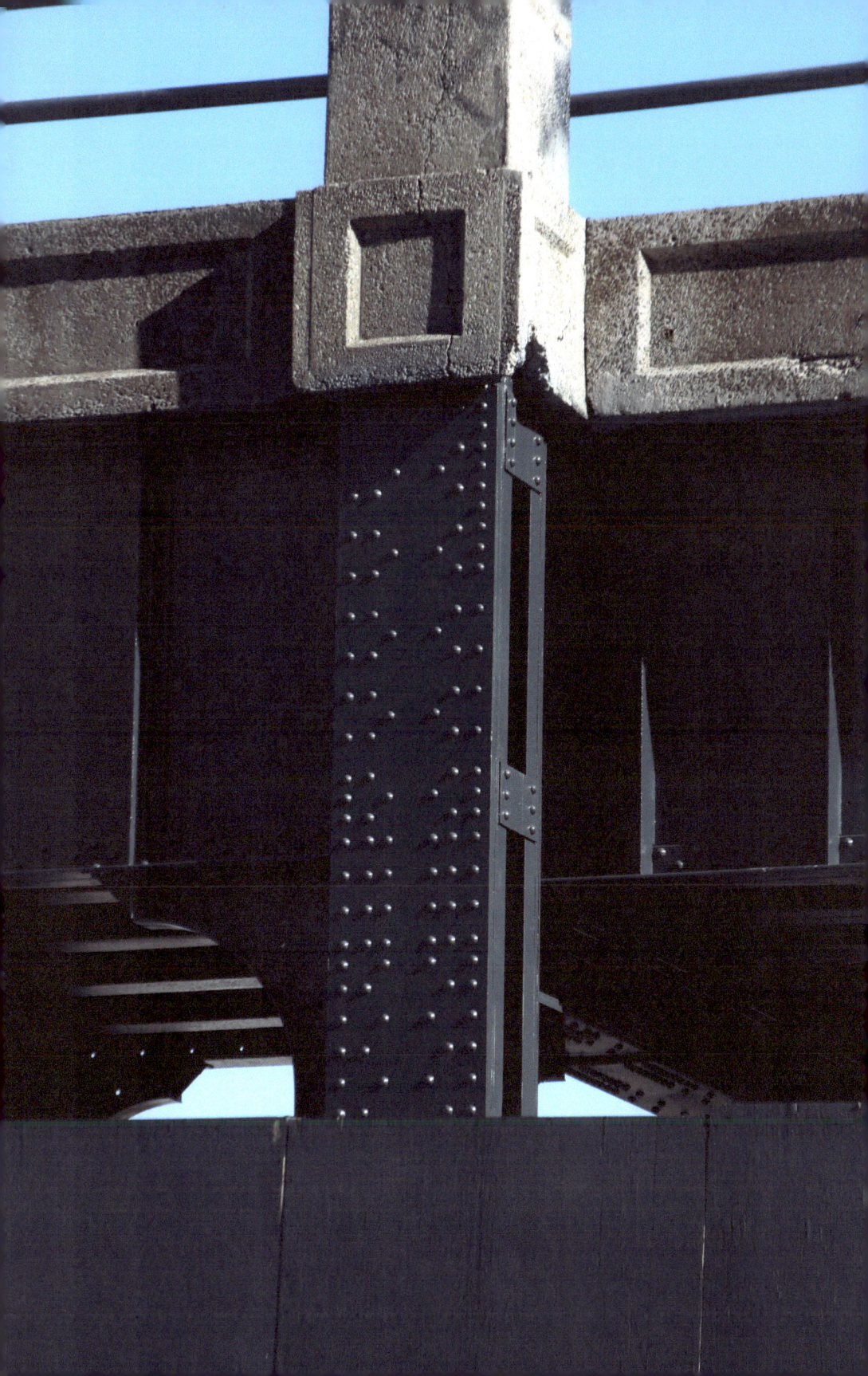

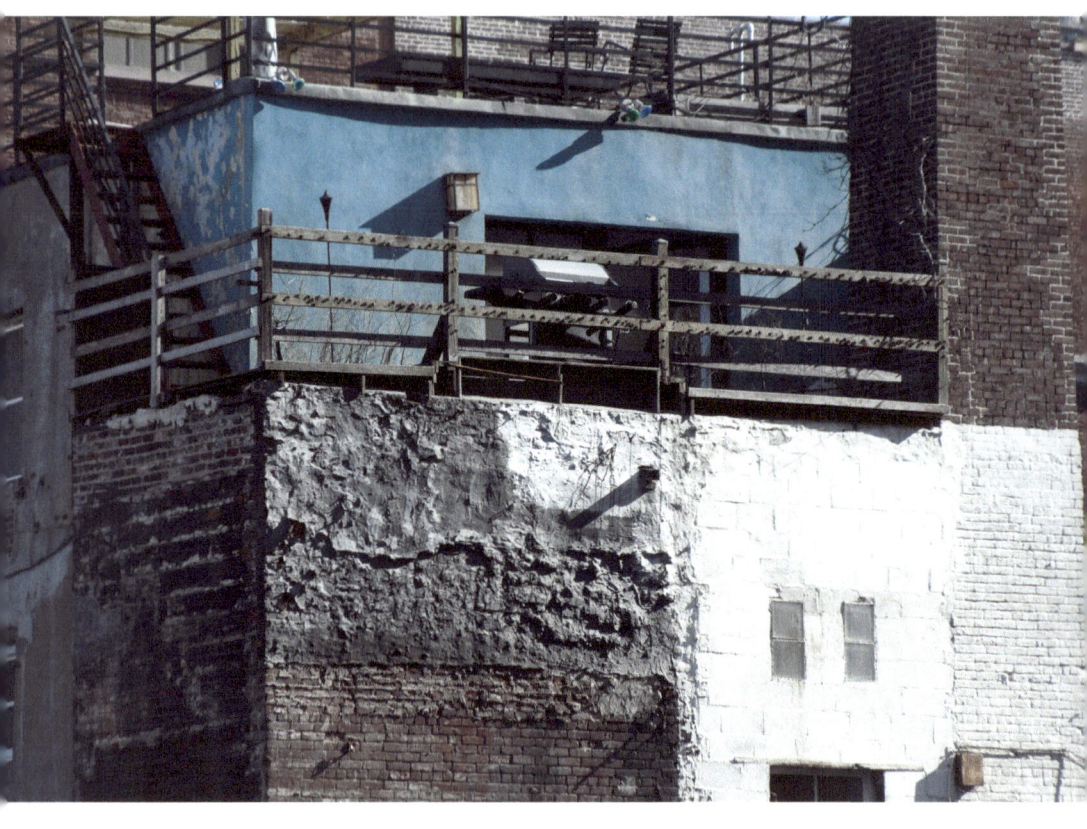

Tevor opened the box and pulled out something he had rarely seen: sheets of paper with handwriting on them. Even his own grandfather had rarely gotten such mail.

"What's that?" Teri asked as she stepped off the elevator.

"Not sure," said Tevor. "We can read it inside."

Normally Tevor would have already started reading the letter aloud, but the top page, in tiny writing, had a warning: "Do not turn to the next page until you are certain no camera can see the contents." He stuffed the letter into a pocket, was cleared by the SecurSweep, and entered the control center with Teri. They relieved the two guards on duty who briefed them and left. Then they were alone for their final shift at the convention.

For a few minutes Tevor and Teri were busy with the routines of a new shift, checking logs and watching the sensors for signs of anomalies, making sure everything was proceeding normally. When they had finished, the vaccinations were still incomplete. It was clear they would take a while more. Tevor pulled the papers out of his pocket. Cameras were everywhere, and it was difficult to find a spot in the room where they couldn't see what was written. But leaning against a wall he turned the page and began reading.

"Electronic communication is compromised," the letter began. "Do not reply except on paper."

Right, Tevor thought. Where would he find paper, except what he held in his hands?

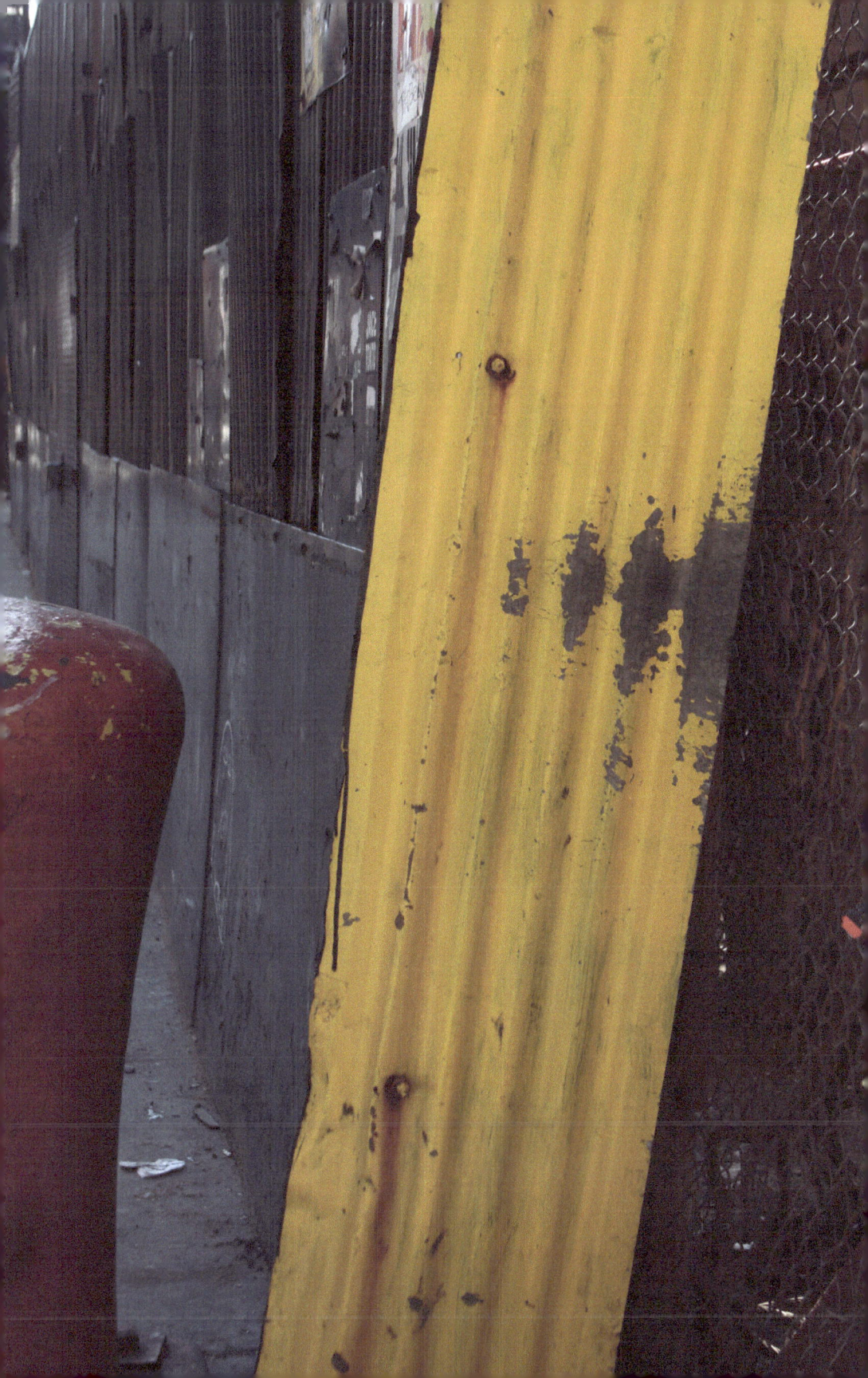

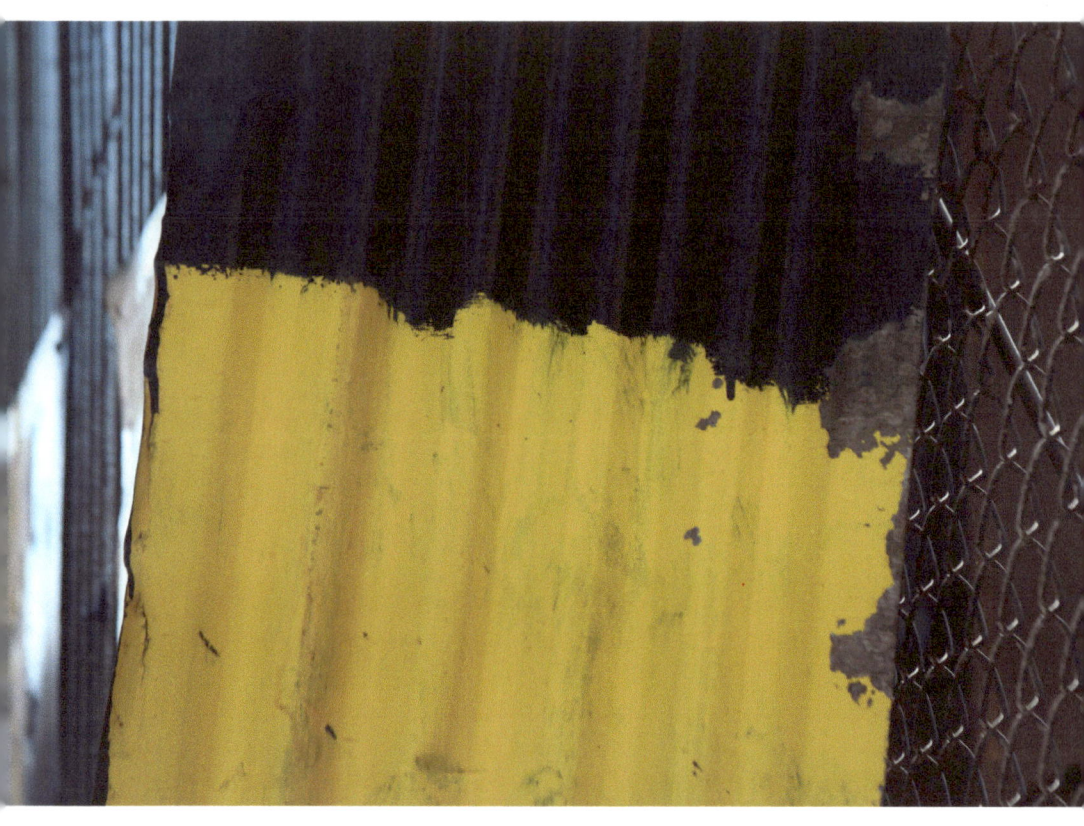

"My name is Jim Blair," the letter said. "I work in Interrogations. I've been trying to call you since the new President's address, but your line has been blocked. In fact, all electronic channels to you are blocked, even though the media embargo is supposed to be over. I finally realized I had to find paper and write."

Tevor looked up. "Teri, have you called anyone this shift? Anyone outside the convention?"

"No. Who would I call? Oh – I know. I could call your mom for you."

"Very funny."

Tevor never called home except in emergencies, and then only when they were over. He'd call his mom himself after the delegates had gone home.

"Call someone besides my mom," he said. "See if the lines are working."

A few seconds later she reported. "All our lines to locations *inside* the convention hall are fine. And I can see plenty of delegates on the convention floor who seem to have gotten a clear signal outside. But our outside lines are still down. They *show* that they're open, but I can't get a signal on any of them."

Tevor returned to the letter.

"Two weeks ago, CentralCommand arrested six handlers from the resistance. They came to Interrogations. We got no information out of five of them. But the sixth was different. He wouldn't stop talking. His name was Robert West. He claimed he had discovered a plot to introduce MalPox to earth. He said a vaccine was being prepared that *caused* the disease instead of preventing it. He said the disease in the vaccine lies dormant until activated by an airport's HealthSweep. As a result, a vaccinated person arrives at the airport healthy, becomes sick on the flight, and dies on arrival, infecting everyone at the destination. Robert gave us detailed information, including the location of the lab making the vaccine."

Tevor rubbed his arm. He had been vaccinated four hours earlier.

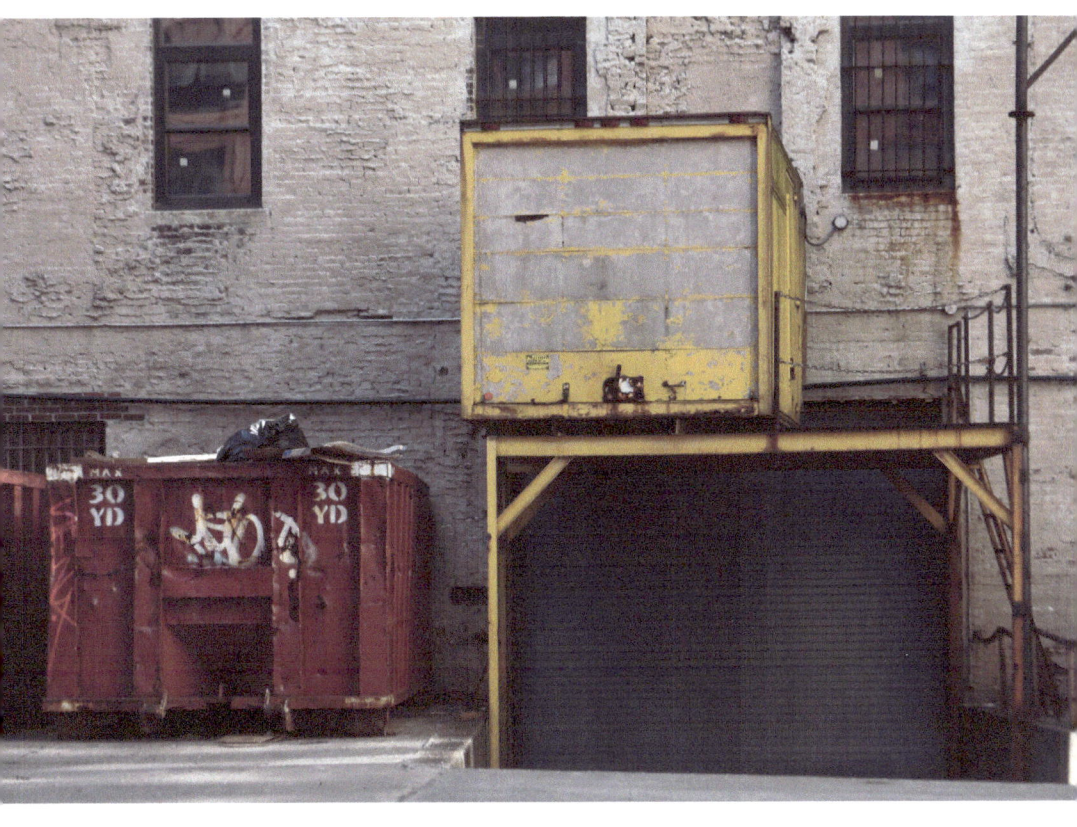

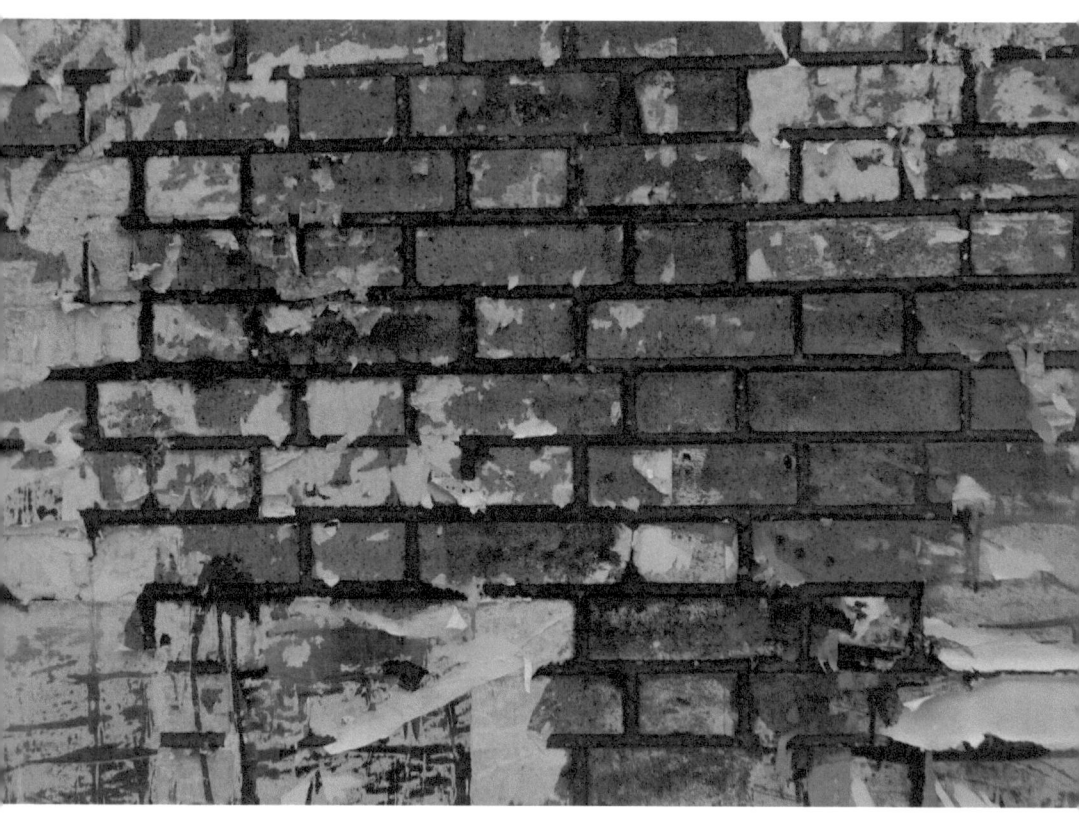

"Robert's information didn't sound realistic to me," Jim wrote. "He seemed too eager to help. None of the other handlers confirmed what he said. But I decided to try to verify some details. I went to the address he gave for the lab.

"It was just an empty storefront. There was no lab.

"By the time I got back to Robert's cell, he was dead. The autopsy found nothing unusual. I filed a report and left it at that.

"Nobody was interested; everyone thought Robert was lying.

"Yesterday, when the new President made his announcement about Whitehorse, the details fit Robert's story. Then the President announced that all the delegates at the convention were getting vaccinations. I looked up who was at ConventionControl and tried calling you but the line went dead. Since then, every phone and ComputAPort I've been near has been broken. I've tried a dozen or more. I've seen people using phones as I approach. By the time I get to them, the machines are inoperable.

"Since it looks like electronic communications are compromised, I found some paper in an antique store and wrote this letter to you.

"P.S. In case you think Robert just saw the news about Whitehorse and made the story up: We arrested Robert several days before anyone died in Whitehorse and more than two weeks before the President made his announcement. I think there's a good chance if the delegates get vaccinated the disease will infect and kill everyone in their home districts."

Tevor sat still. The delegates at the convention included observers from nearly every location on earth – for that matter, nearly every location in the system except Santori Ten.

The letter could be just a gag. But if electronic communications *were* compromised, he couldn't discuss anything out loud with Teri.

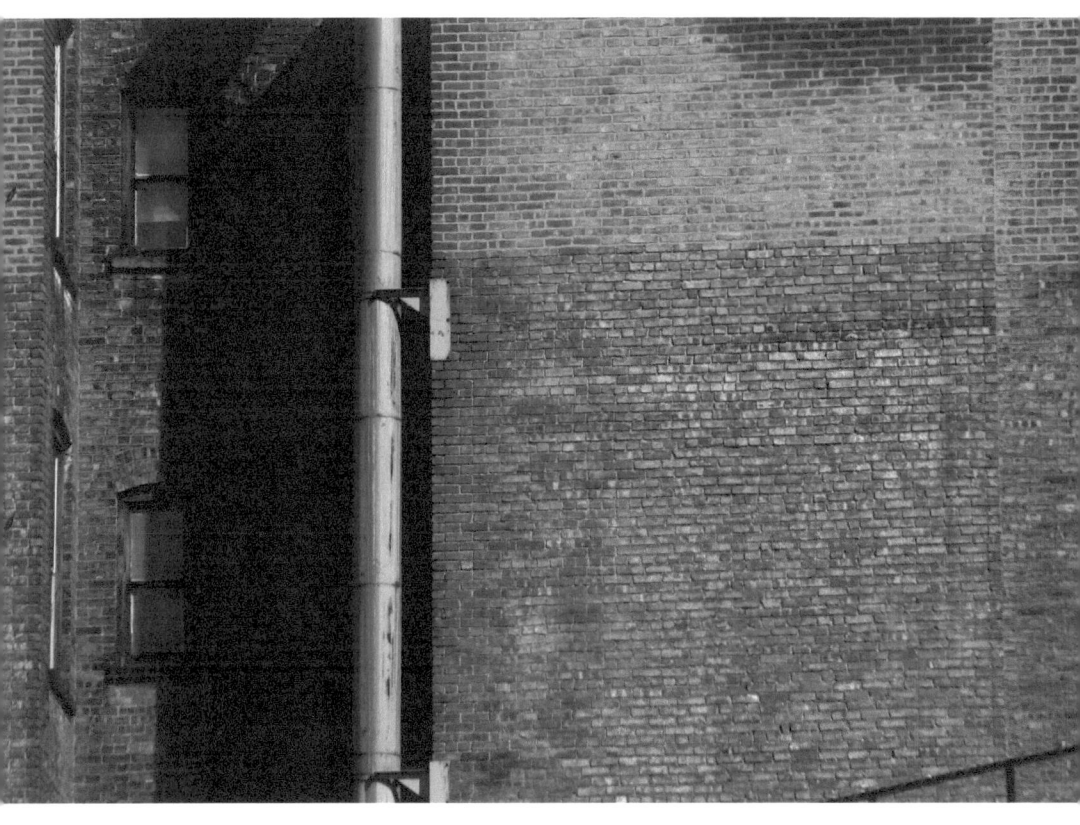

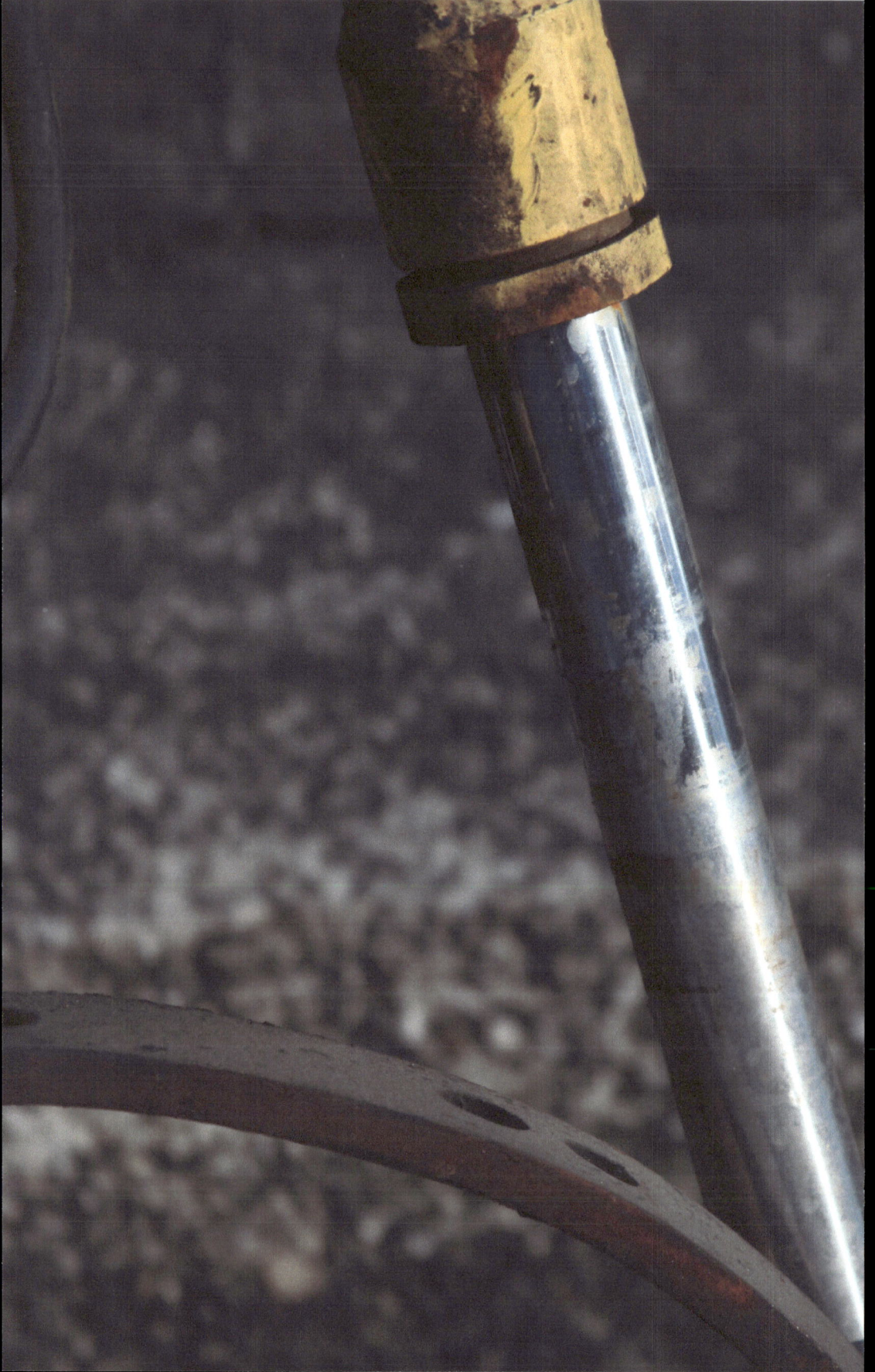

On the monitors, about ninety percent of the delegates were already in the banquet hall.

About ninety percent vaccinated, Tevor thought. The remaining delegates were receiving vaccinations in a steady stream. At one end of the hall, servers were already bringing food to those who had been seated first. In less than forty minutes everyone would be heading home.

"Hey Teri," Tevor said. "A friend of mine knew this shift might be boring and sent a game. Grab a pencil and come over here."

"A game? Now? And anyway, where would I find a pencil? Who keeps one of *those*?"

"They're in the back of the supply closet. It'll be a while before we have to do anything to wrap up. Go get one. Let's try this."

Teri glanced at the monitors. The delegates would be eating for another fifteen minutes. It was unlikely there would be anything of interest for her to do during that time. But still. A game, when they were supposed to be working?

Ten days earlier, she would have said "No." But in the crises of the past ten days she had learned to trust Tevor. So she found a pencil and sat next to him. Tevor took the pencil and wrote, "Just smile and play along."

Out loud he said, "Read the rules first, then we'll play."

Teri read the letter, her eyes slightly widening. "You start," she said when she had finished.

"I hope this is a hoax," Tevor wrote. "But if it's true, by tomorrow most of the people on the planet will be dead."

"If we tell delegates they have to stay longer while we check this out, we'll have a mutiny," Teri wrote.

"We can't run queries on the NewsGraph," Tevor wrote. "If communications are compromised we wouldn't know what to trust."

Teri paused. She didn't like what she was going to propose. But she could think of nothing else.

"Pick a region you don't care about," she wrote. "Let a few delegates from there go home first. Have everyone watch on a live feed. If the delegates die of MalPox, everyone else will be willing to listen to a plan that requires them to stay longer. If it's a hoax, the first group will arrive safely and you can let everyone else go home."

"Can we get a live feed?"

Teri shrugged. It was possible there was no way to win this game. "We have to test the threat somehow," she wrote.

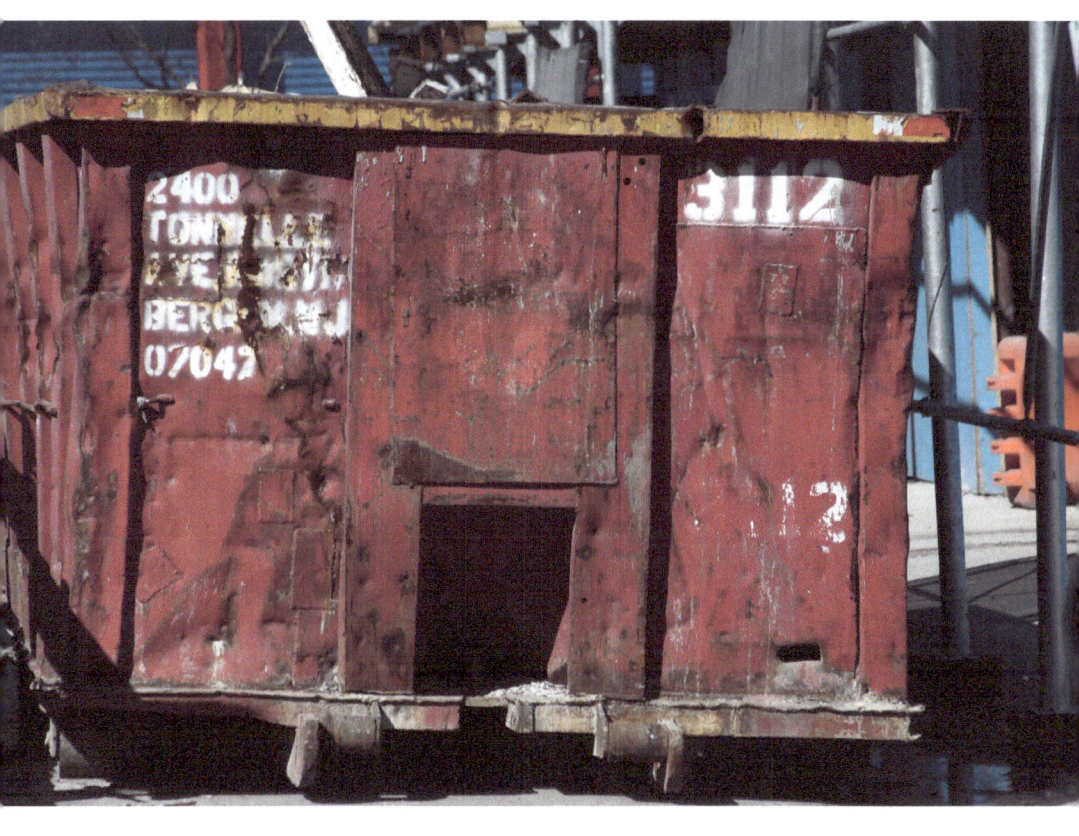

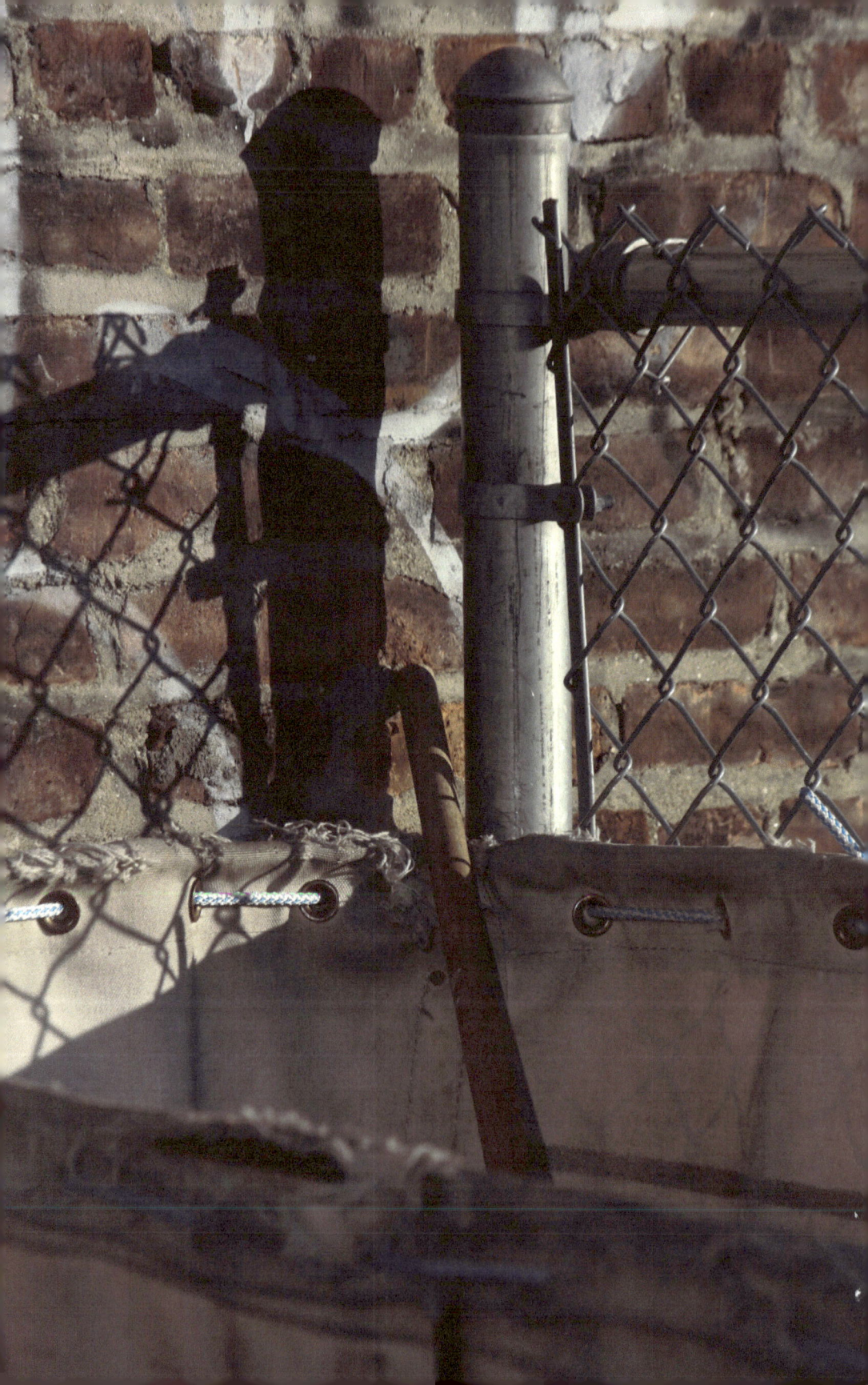

"What location is that isolated?" Tevor wrote. "It would have to be an island."

"Guam? Hawaii? Santori Ten. . . "

"No. There's military and industry at each of those that we don't want to lose," Tevor wrote. He called up a map by habit before remembering not to trust electronic communications.

He stared at the map, looking for locations. "Juneau is compromised by the radiation," he wrote. "They haven't announced yet how bad it is. We could have Juneau's bridge to the mainland blown up."

"Do we *have* delegates from Juneau?"

"Alaska has three. Only one is from the old capitol. But we could route them all through it anyway. They can get anywhere in the state from there."

"Okay," Teri wrote. "Got a better plan?"

"Not in the time we've got."

"If the letter is right, you're going to lose Juneau."

"We'll be lucky if that's all we lose," Tevor wrote.

Out loud, Tevor said, "Great game. Now back to work." He folded the papers and stuffed them into his pocket.

Tevor could think of no way around it: If communications were compromised, their plan would be revealed as soon as they started to implement it. So he held off as long as he could.

When the President was almost done speaking, Tevor ported the three Alaska delegates and a media crew to the airport Tube. He noticed happily that several outside communication lines had become available, including a live feed. Tevor sent the Alaska delegates and the news crew explanations of the plan.

If communications were compromised, whoever was behind the plot would know that the vaccine's deadly nature would be revealed by the Juneau flight. But Tevor hoped they couldn't act fast enough to stop it.

A minute later the new President finished a rousing speech and the images on the monitors in the hall switched to the flight arriving in Juneau.

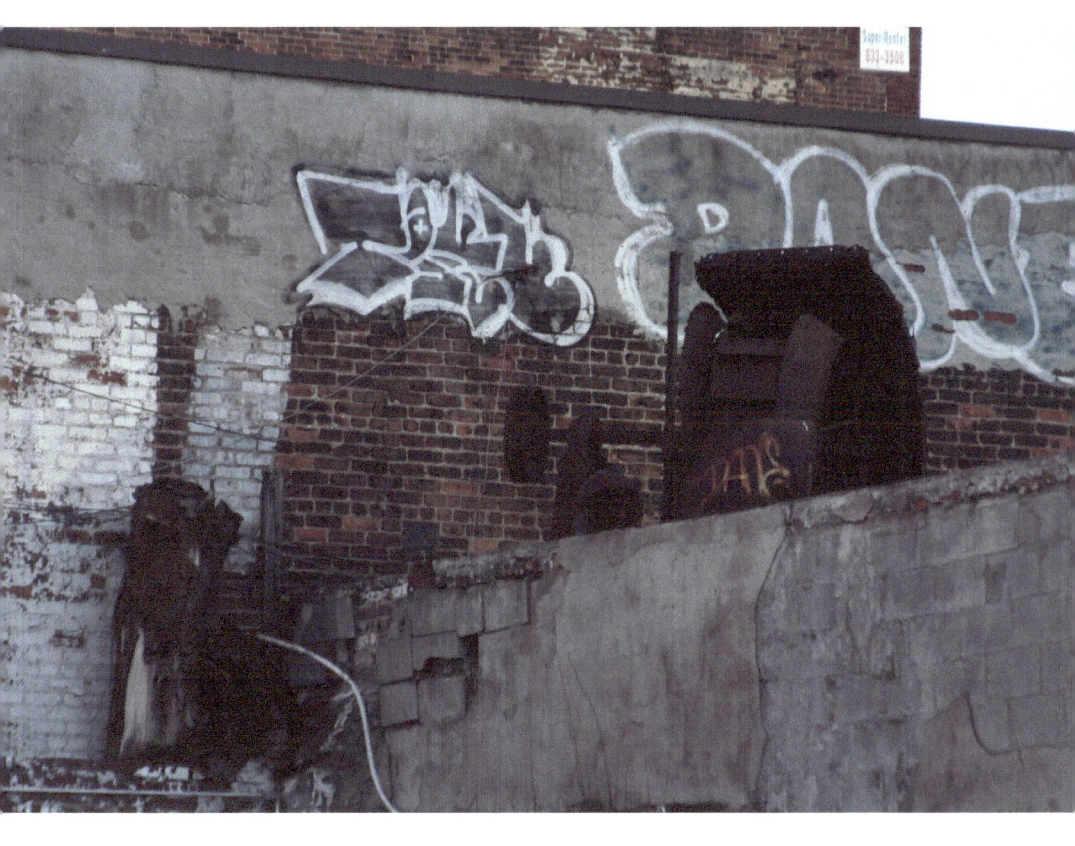

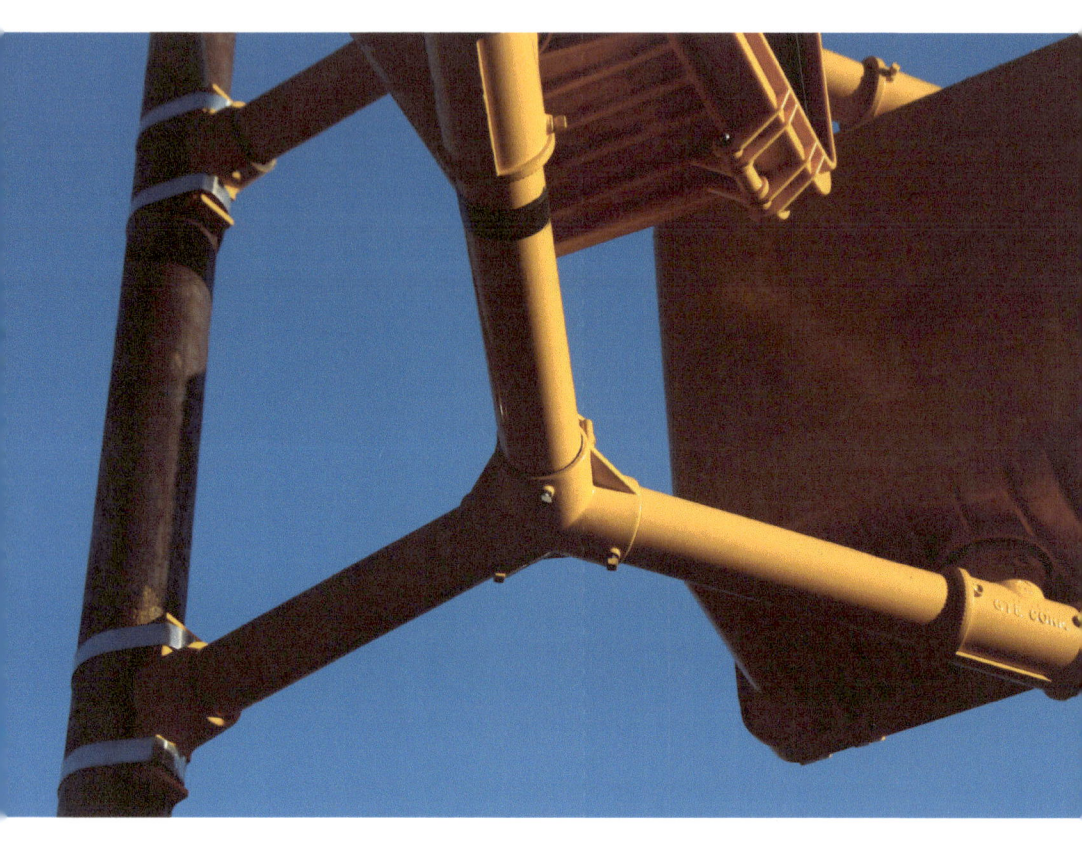

Jazreene, one of the Alaska delegates, turned to face the camera. Her smiling face filled the screens of the convention center.

"We've still got lots of work to do," she said, reading her lines off a prompt. "Juneau will have to be evacuated soon because of the radiation from Whitehorse. In your district, you will face challenges, too. But the Otto Party has prevailed in the past, and we can prevail now."

Balloons and confetti started falling on the delegates, signaling the end of the convention. The delegates in the hall rose to their feet, cheering, and the band began playing the party theme song. All the delegates sang about the bright future ahead, and the monitors in the convention hall switched to images of their revelry.

Tevor absentmindedly tapped the pencil against a table. He was still watching the Juneau feed. Everything seemed normal. No MalPox outbreak.

It seemed too easy.

Tevor didn't *want* the letter to be real. But he was surprised nothing had happened.

After two minutes had gone by, there was no reason he could see to stop the end of the convention.

A minute later, the delegates were streaming out the doors of the banquet hall, on their way to tubes and airports, hailing ShuttleCabs, and using a thousand routes to try to beat the crowds and get home first.

"Okay to sign off?" asked a camera operator on the Juneau team. Five minutes had elapsed. MalPox always presented within the first sixty seconds, so Tevor could find no reason to wait any more.

"Sure," said Tevor. "Thanks. Have a safe flight home."

The feed went black.

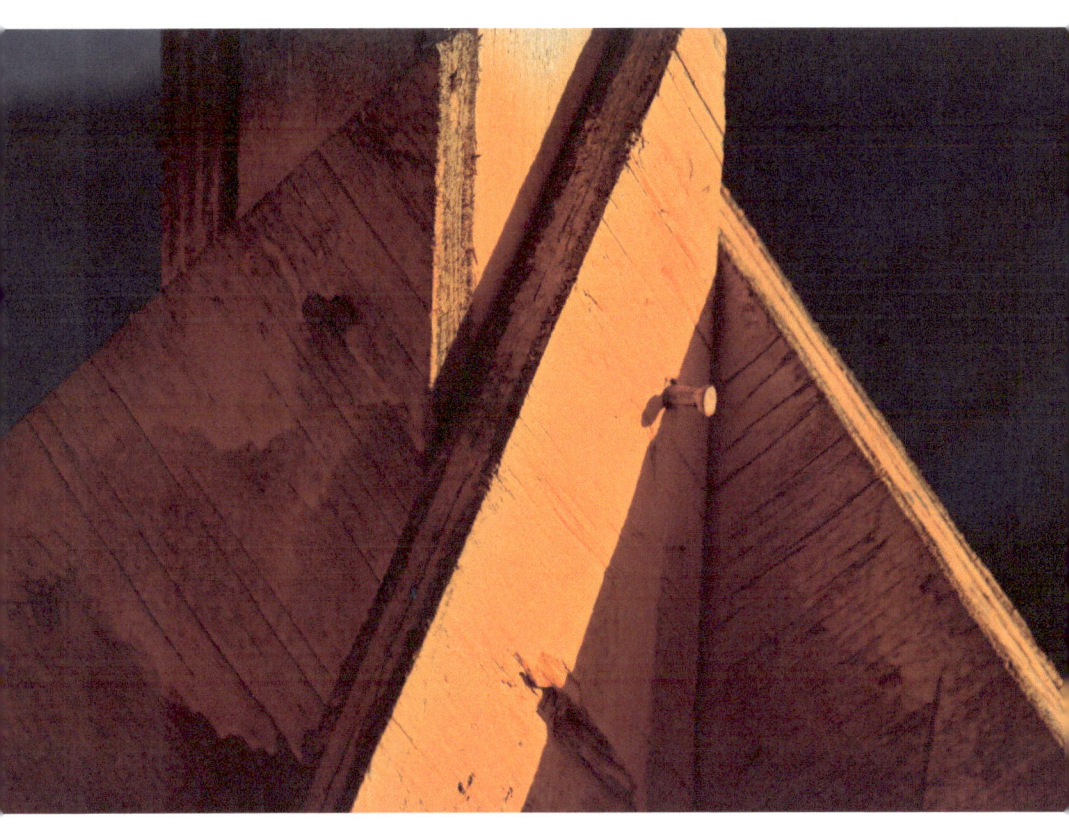

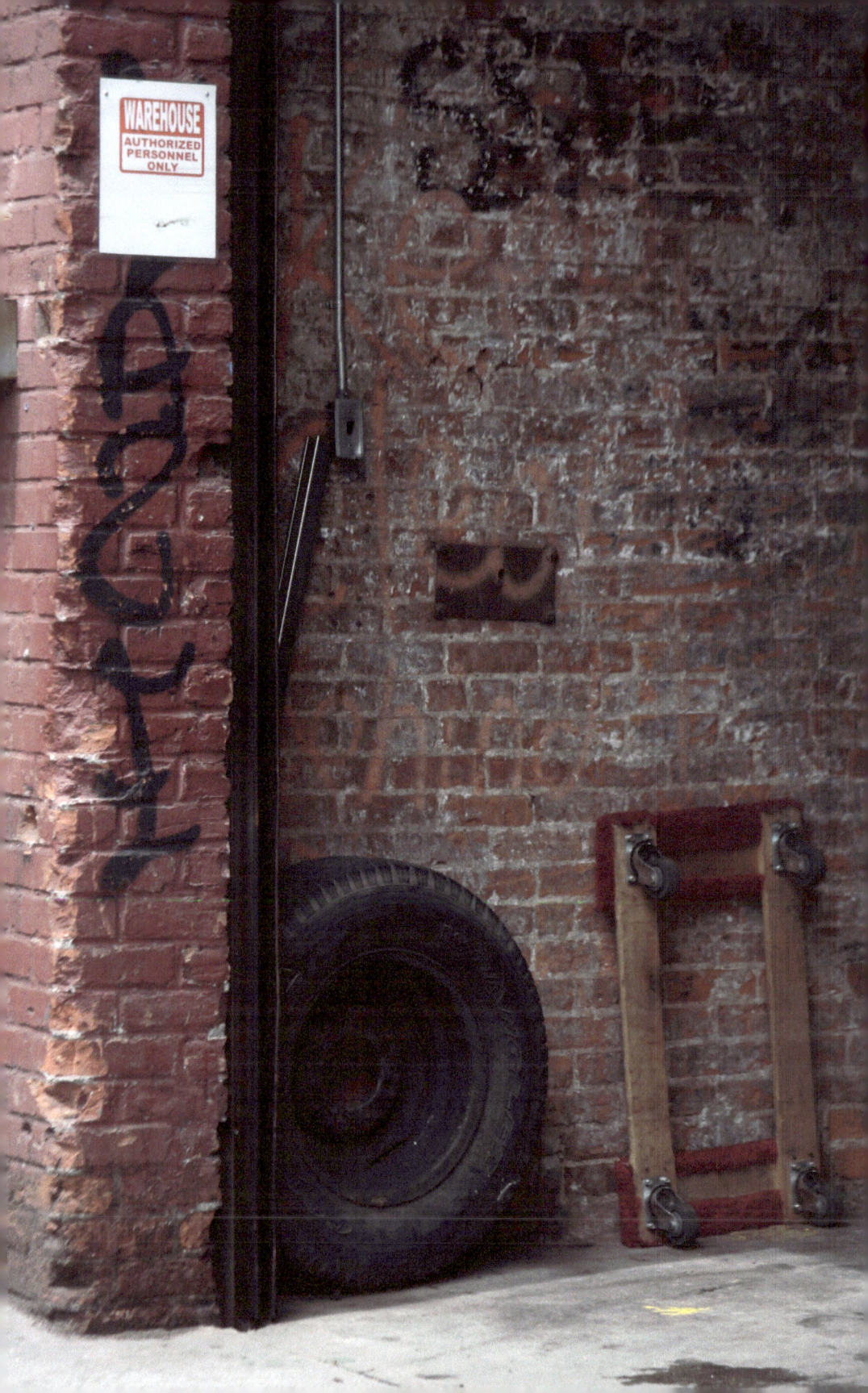

Inside the Juneau airport a chime sounded.

> * Attention passengers. A HealthSweep of the entire
> terminal will commence in ten seconds. Please stand still.

The passengers looked at each other. Normally HealthSweeps were only done immediately *before* a flight. But security regulations were constantly changing, and most in the airport figured this was just another such change. The lights dimmed and came back on.

Jazreene waved goodbye to Nolee. She scanned the area but couldn't see Stan, the third delegate.

"See you at the next convention," she said. She took a step toward the exit, wobbling slightly. A puzzled look came to her face, and she touched her throat and coughed.

Back in the convention's security room, Teri and Tevor were wrapping up, filling out logs. Teri looked up with surprise, seeing one of the reports.

"Did the HealthScan run before the Juneau flight?" she asked.

"It's automatic. It always runs. Why do you ask?"

"There is a report here from the HealthLab. Stan Tarney, one of the Alaska delegates, showed up last night at MedicRelief with a fever. But he refused treatment. He was determined to go home, where he could talk to his regular AutoDoc."

"He must have recovered."

"Maybe. But I didn't see anyone else being removed from the flight. How often does that happen – that 100 percent of the passengers make it through a HealthScan?"

"It never happens."

"Right. But it did on the live feed we just watched."

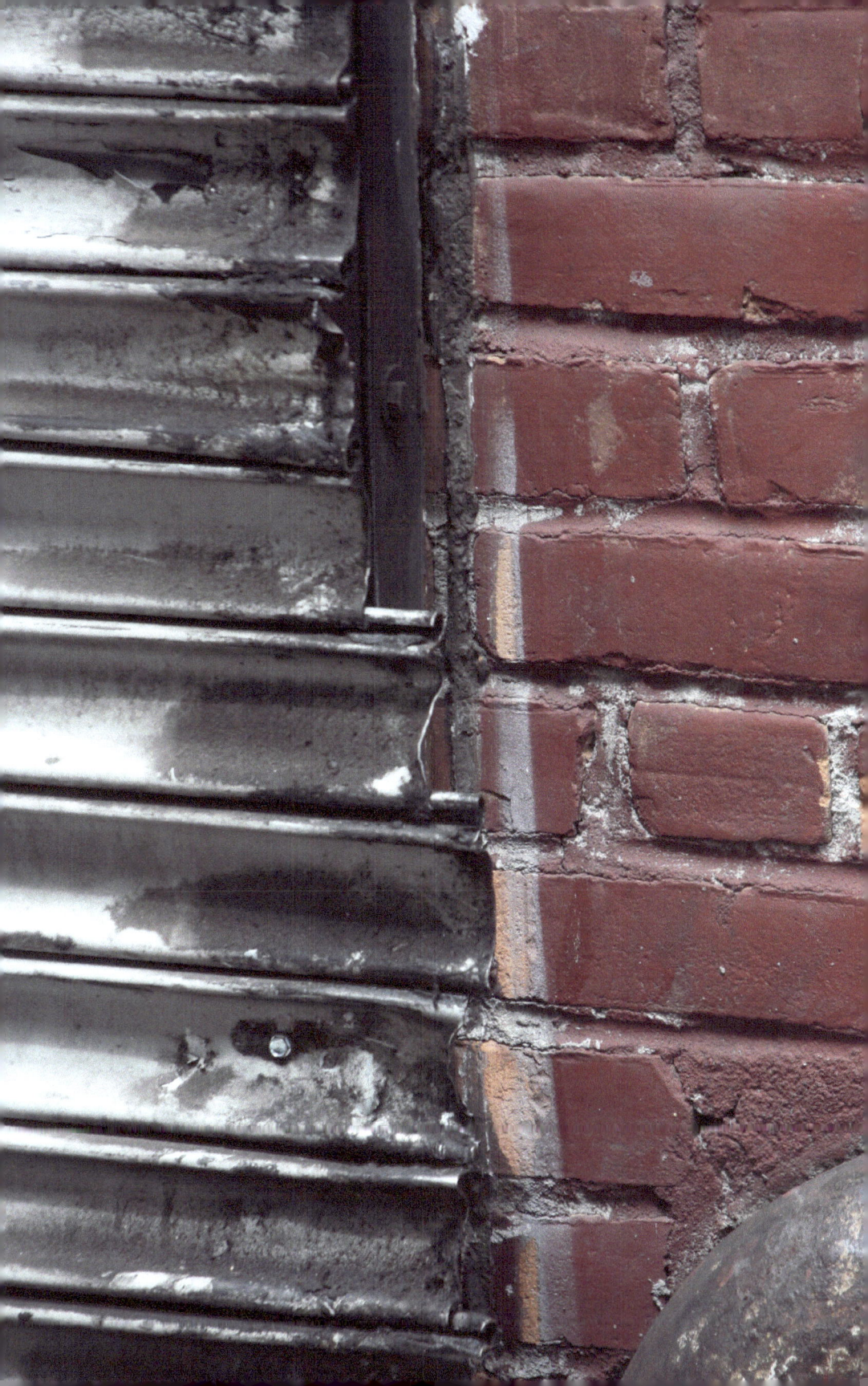

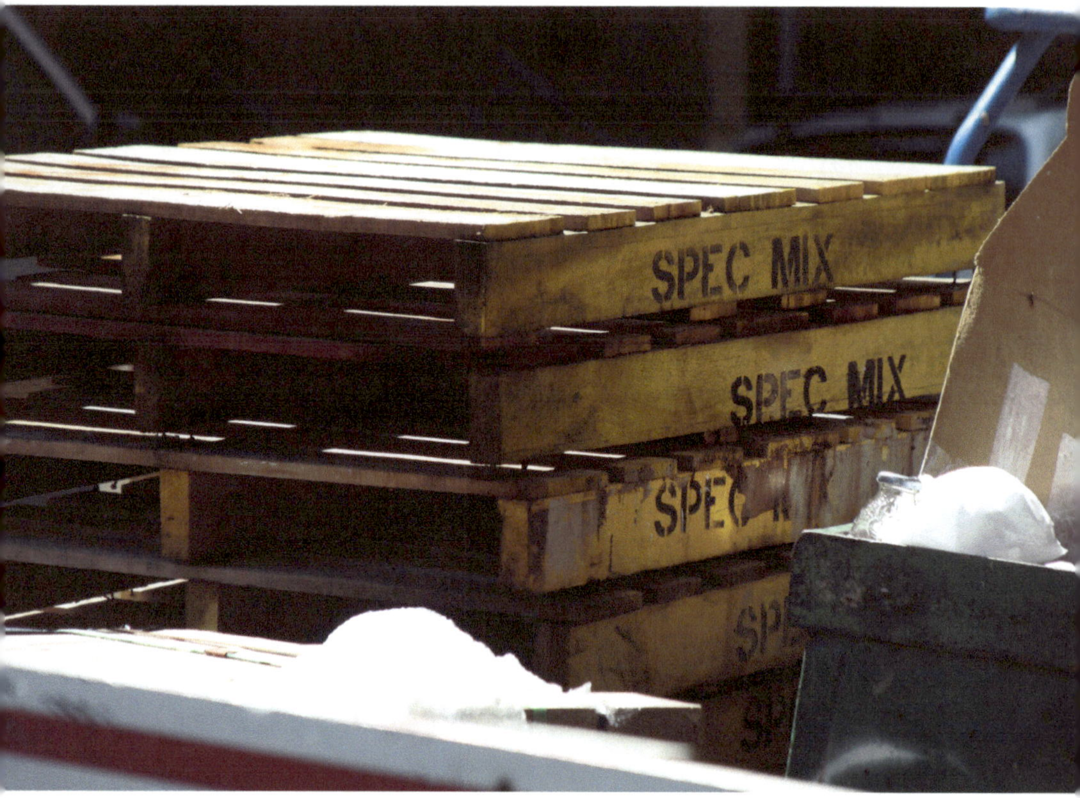
SPEC MIX
SPEC MIX

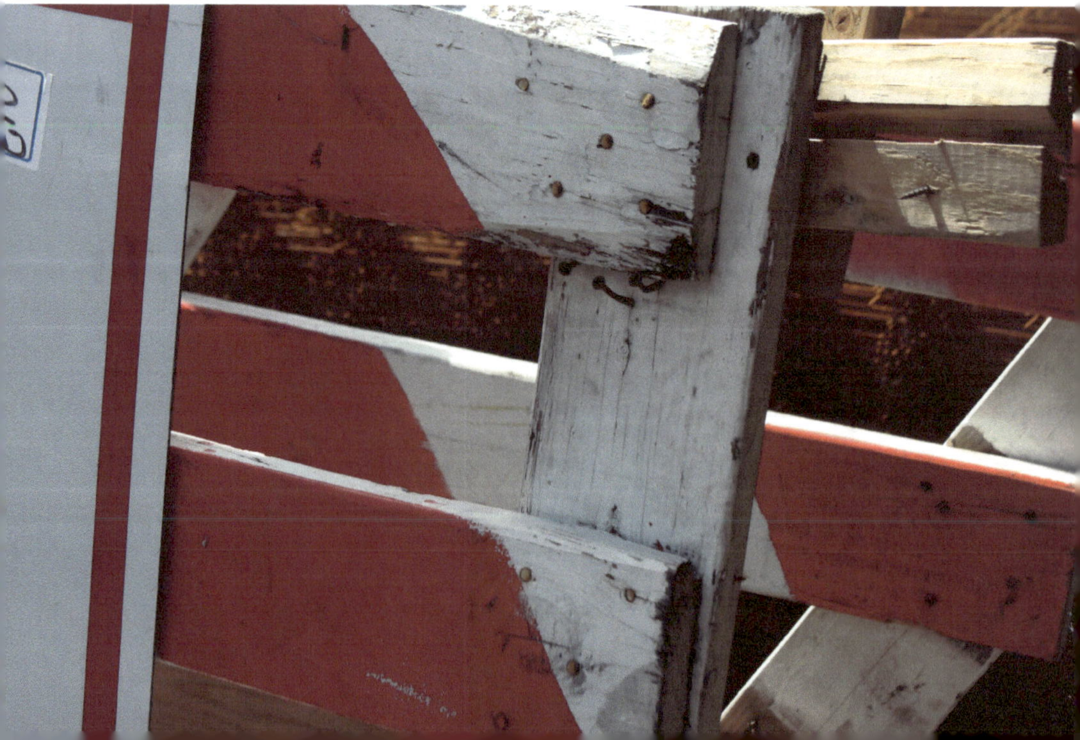

Tevor activated his clearance and checked the airport's flight log. Teri was right. For some reason the HealthScan had not run. On the live video feed of the Juneau flight, Tevor had seen the lights dim and then be restored. But something else had caused the lights to dim – it wasn't the HealthScan. None of the passengers had been screened. Tevor and Teri still had not watched a real test of the vaccine.

Tevor groaned. There was no way all the delegates could be recalled at this point. Some would have already left for home on the Duluth Tube; others would be arriving for flights at the Chicago Minnesota airport within minutes; others would already be on HeliPorts. . . .

As he stared at the banks of monitors showing nearly empty halls, Tevor thought about thousands of people returning to thousands of locations via thousands of routes. Then two things happened, nearly in the same instant.

First, his computer screen suddenly changed.

It now reported that the HealthScan had run, and gave complete reports on the health of passengers on the Juneau flight.

And second, his NewsGraph indicated an incoming message from an unidentified line. Tevor had never heard of an unidentified line. Teri received the same message. They both answered at the same time.

"Hello, Tevor and Teri," said a voice. "I have some bad news that I am hoping you can help us with. Don't talk; just listen. Everything around you is monitored. At the moment, this communication is safe if you just listen.

"There was no HealthScan before the Juneau flight. All the documents that just popped onto Tevor's screen have been manufactured to hide that fact.

"The danger to the delegates who are leaving the convention is real; as soon as they go through a HealthScan, MalPox will be released and the flights they are on will become infected. Within a few hours, most of the people on the planet will be dying. We need your help to save as many as we can. Your vaccination and the vaccinations of a few other delegates were placebos. It was the best we could do."

For the next few minutes Tevor and Teri followed instructions from someone they didn't know. They ported specific individuals still in the banquet hall to a local business two blocks away.

Someone with a lower security clearance might have stuck with protocols and refused, but the point of having Tevor and Teri in place was that they could make decisions like this. And they both figured in this case the stakes justified the risk. If they were fired, they were fired.

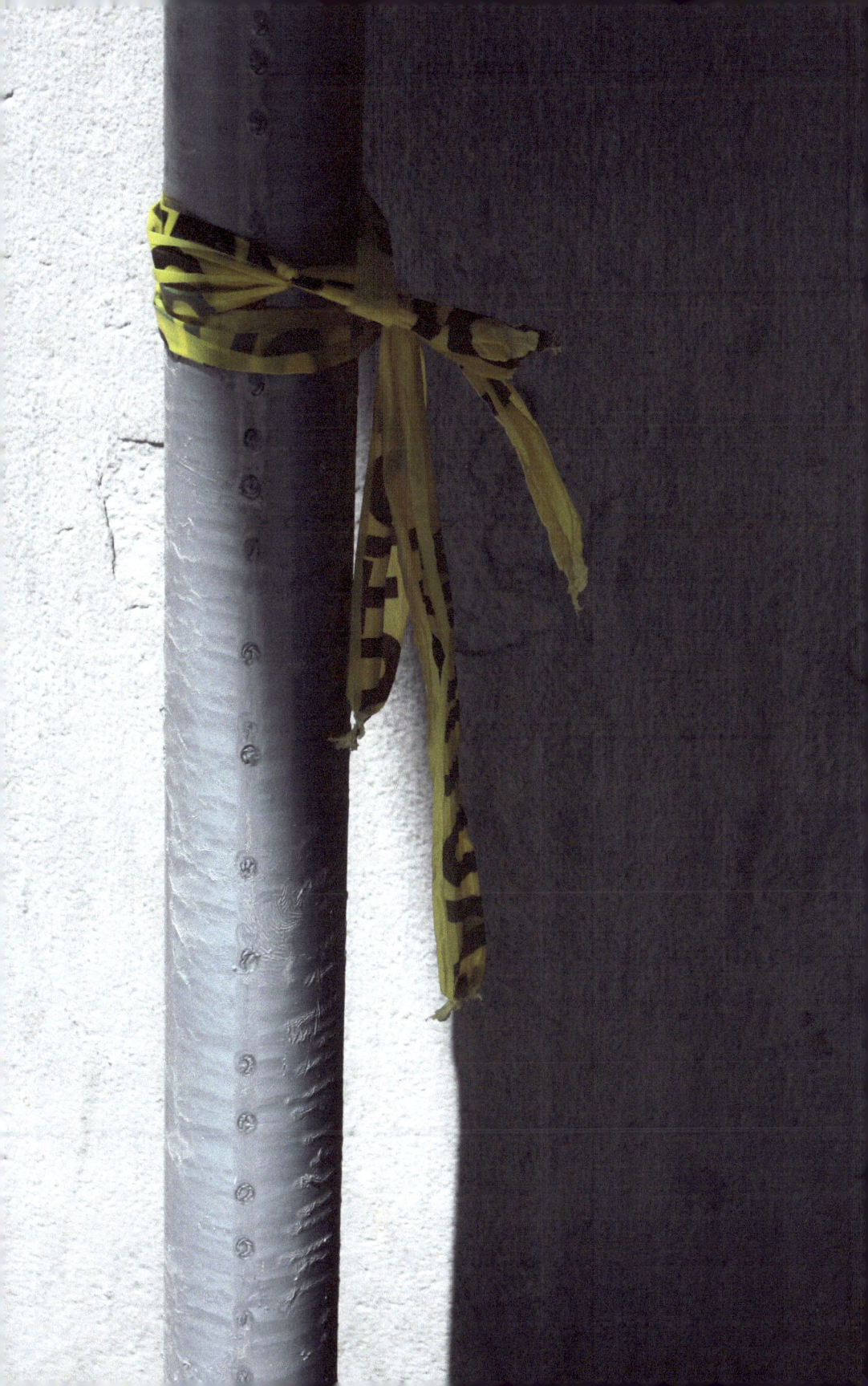

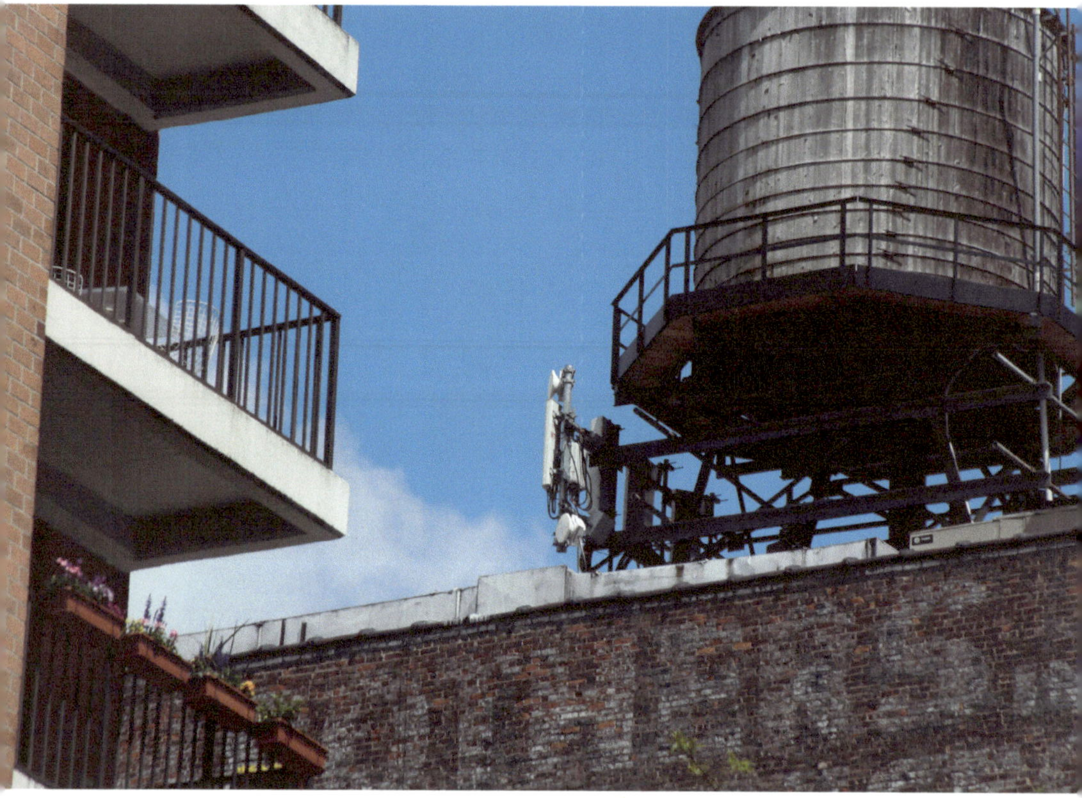

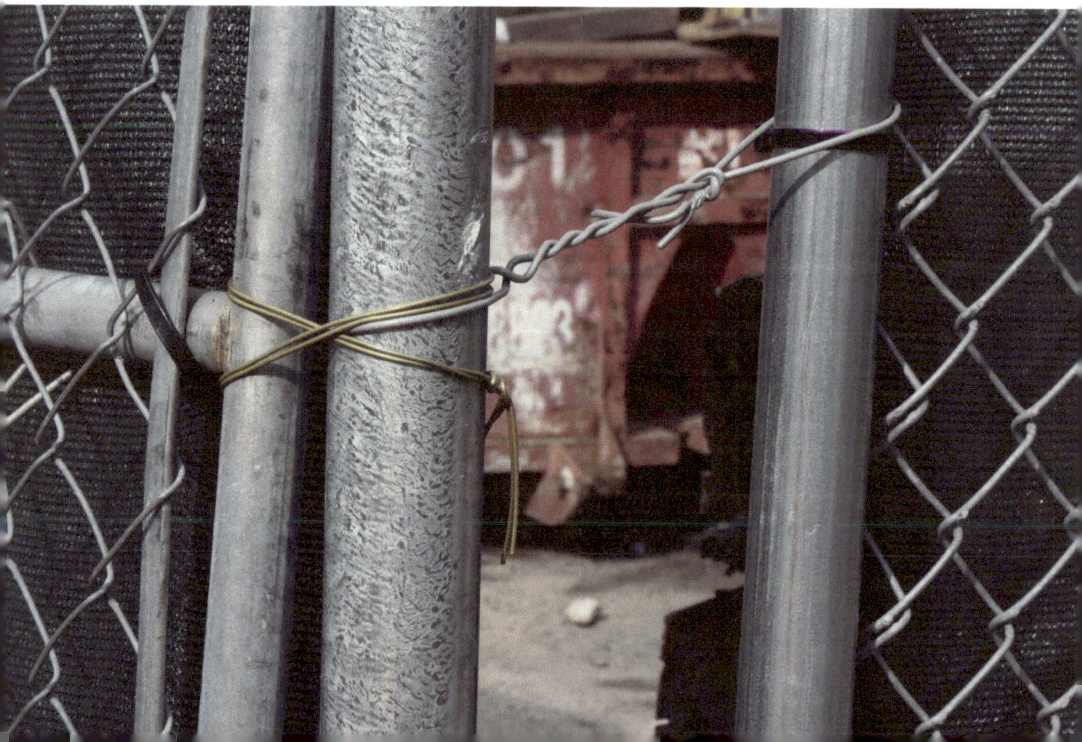

In the middle of transporting the twentieth individual, the port unexpectedly jammed.

"Okay," said the voice on the phone. "We've been discovered. That's all we can rescue. Your turn. Don't move."

Tevor and Teri felt themselves being ported. A few seconds later, they were in a reception area of that same local business. Ten of the people they had ported were still there.

A voice on the loudspeaker said, "We're sorry how inconvenient this will be for you. We're not sure we can get your luggage to you. The group that just left has been sent to Iceland. They only have a ten percent chance of survival, but we wanted to try someplace on earth. The odds of *your* survival are slightly greater. But to get those odds, we have to send you off planet.

"Don't move for the transfer. For your safety, and we hope for the safety of humanity, you are being sent to Santori Ten."

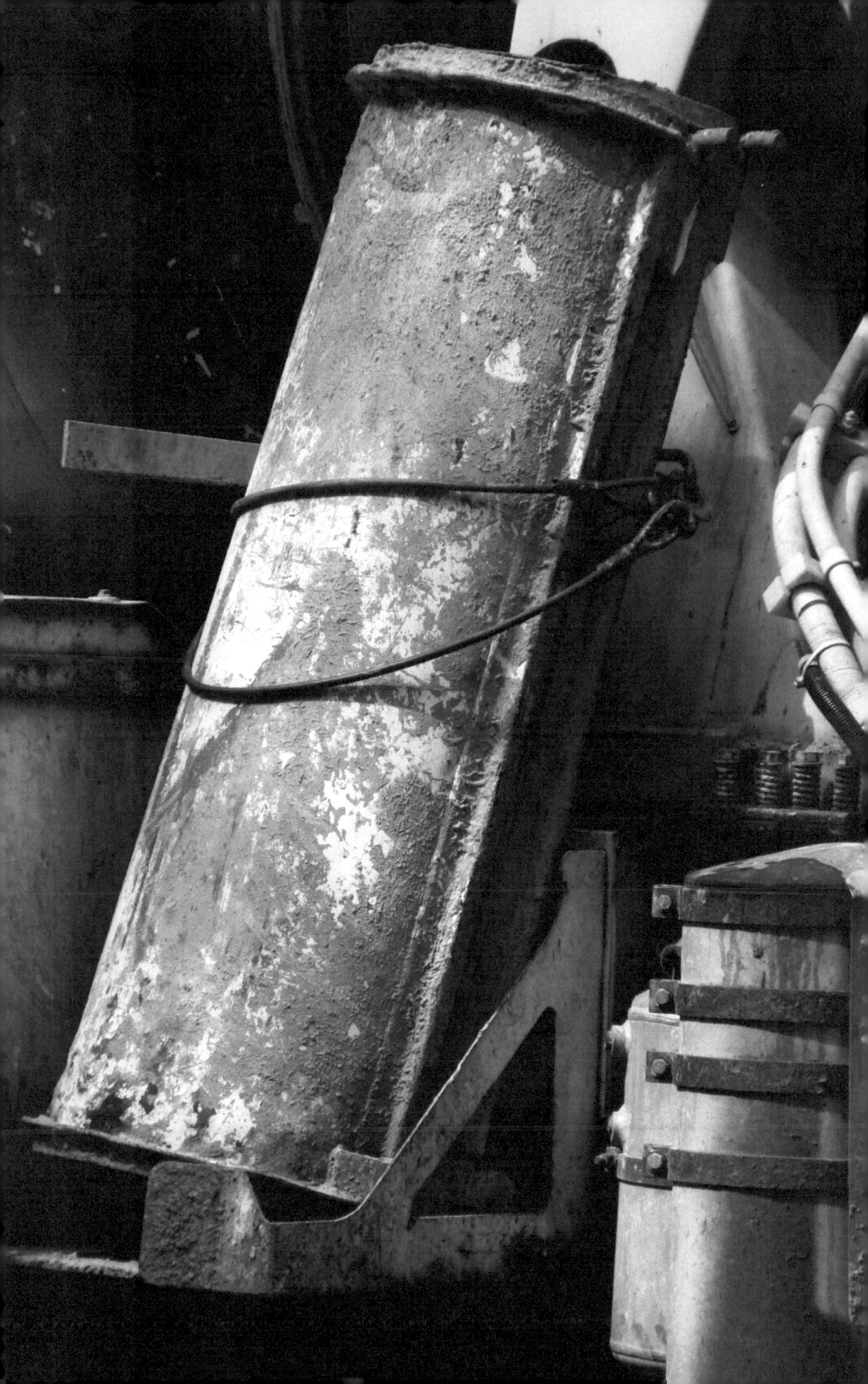

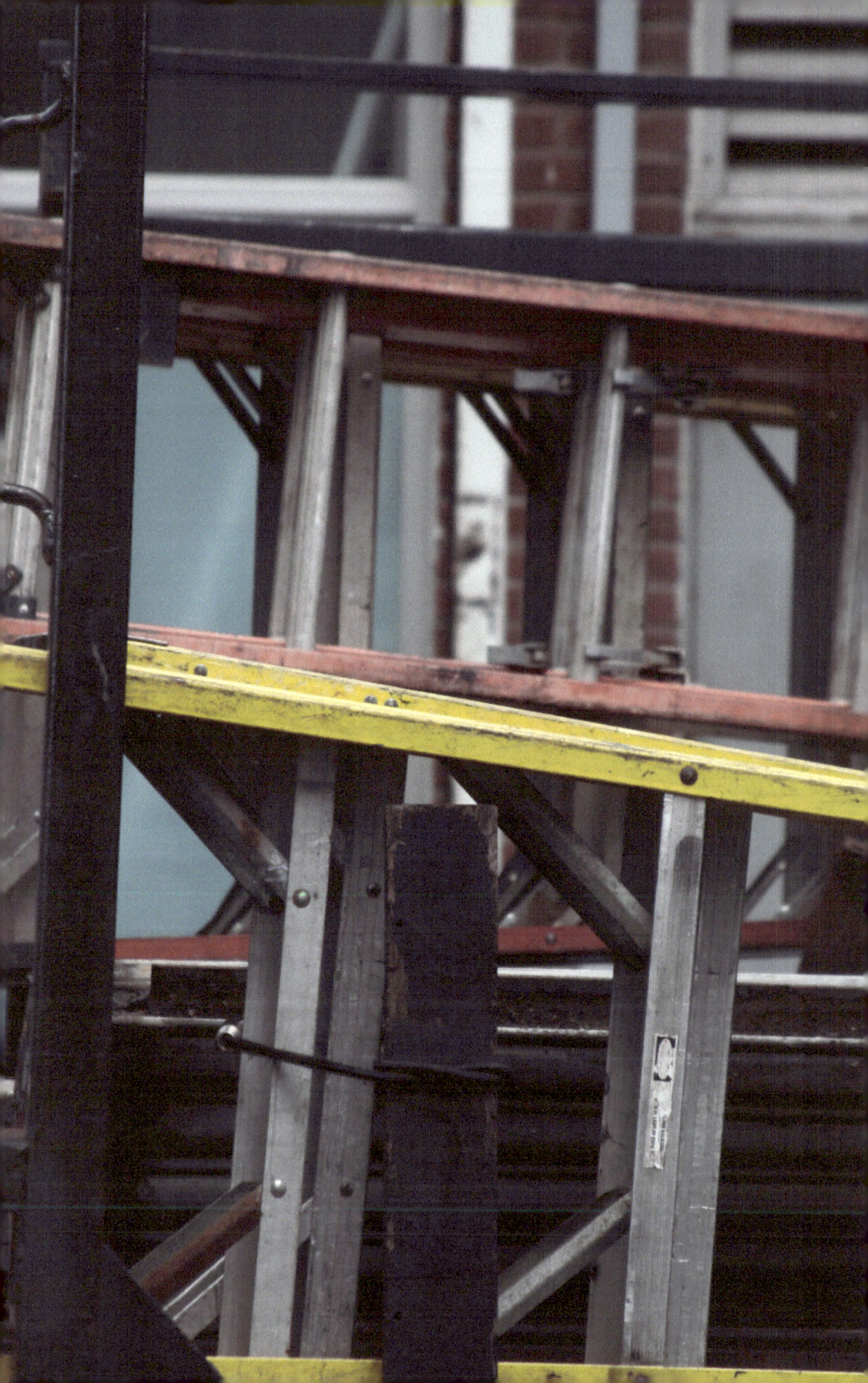

Panic filled the eyes of the few delegates who comprehended what it would be like to arrive on Santori Ten with no preparations: no gas mask, no HeatShield, no LiquiLite.

Tevor and Teri knew one other fact, since the inbound flight for Santori Ten delegates had been cancelled at the last minute: Friz had already ended, and all legal flights had been suspended until at least March. They would be arriving by unregistered carrier in the summer months.

Then the transfer started.

The voice continued during transfer.

"Within an hour, those who want humans exterminated on earth will mostly have gotten their wish. But a few of us like your species. We have a special fondness for how slow you are and how fragile. We will do our best to care for you."

The transfer ended, with fewer jolts than might have been expected, given that Friz had ended. The doors opened, and the suffocating air and blistering heat from Santori Ten flooded the room. A new day had begun. The delegates were home.

~~

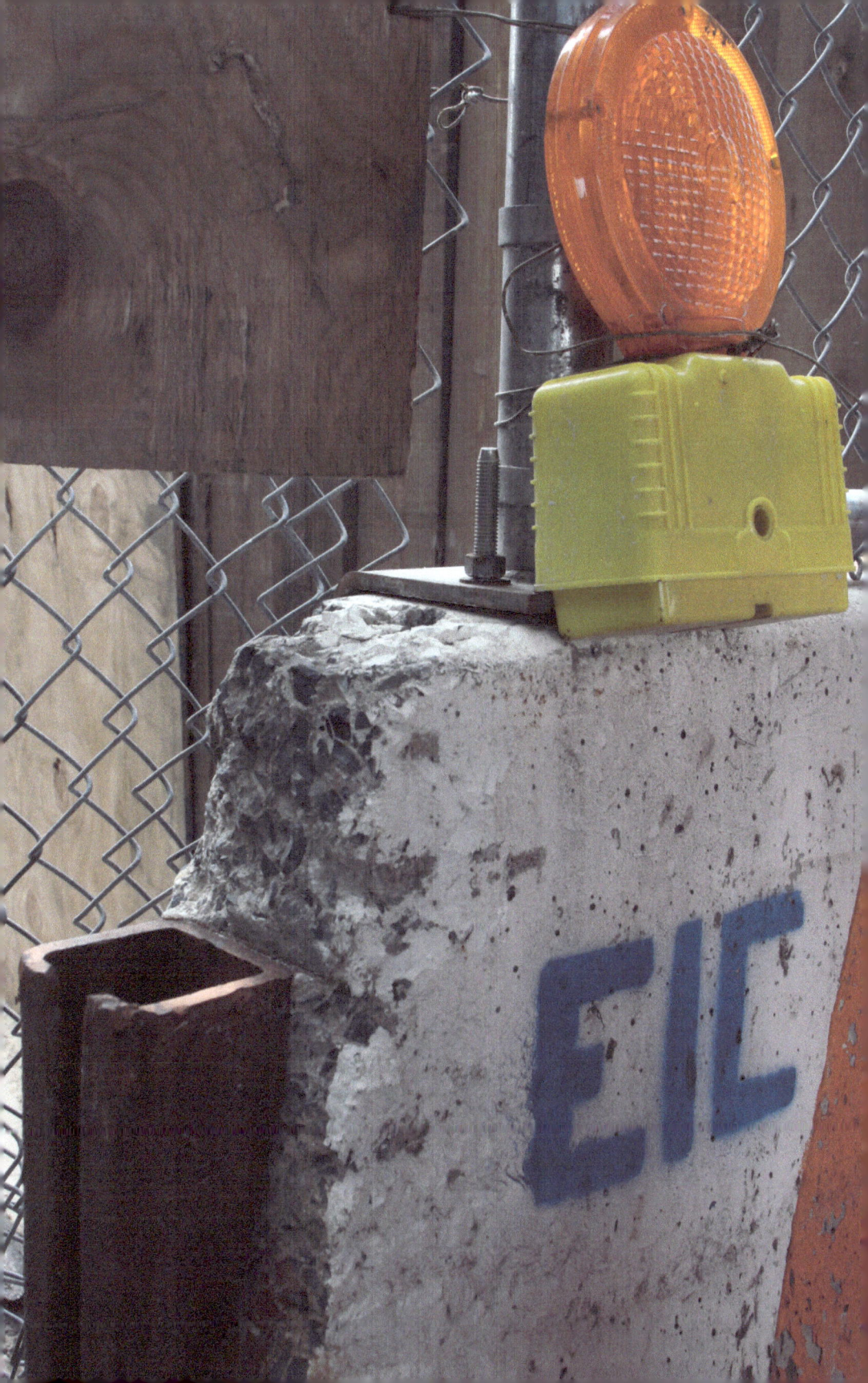

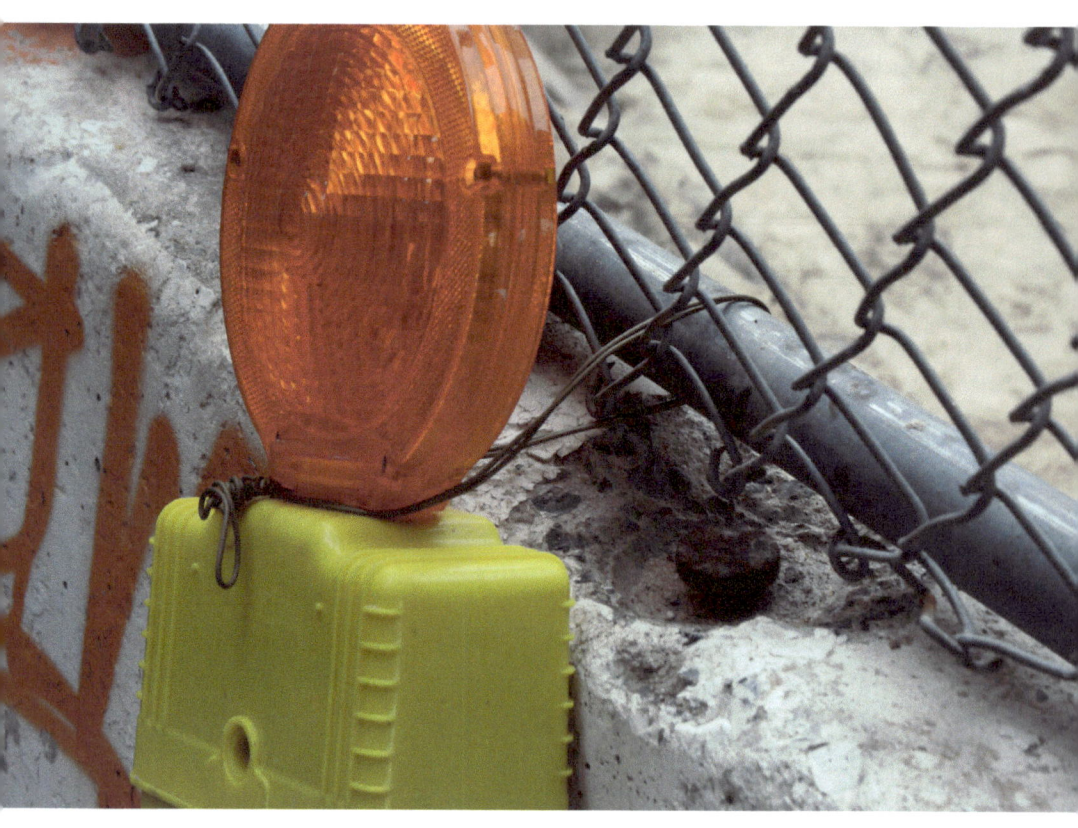

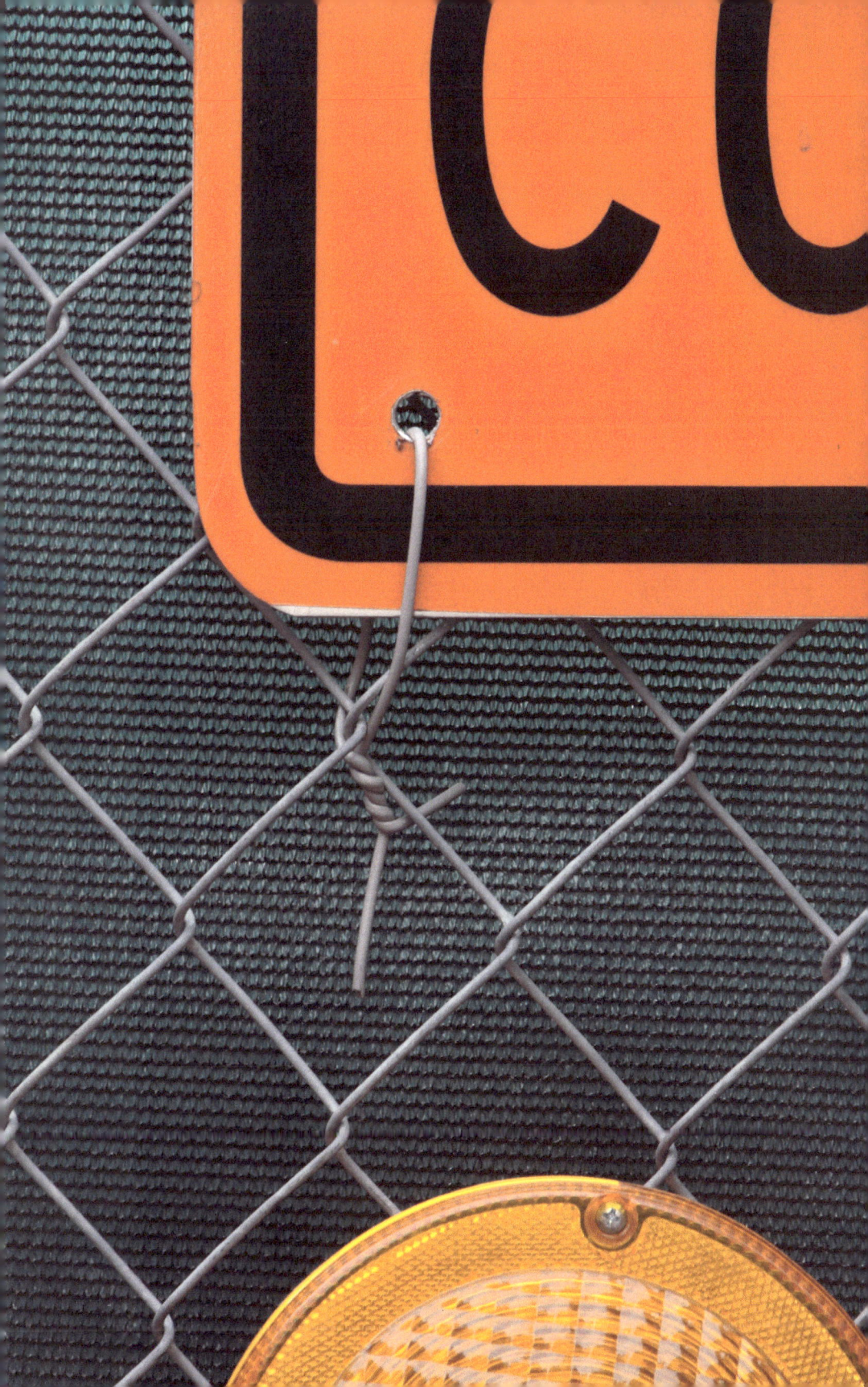

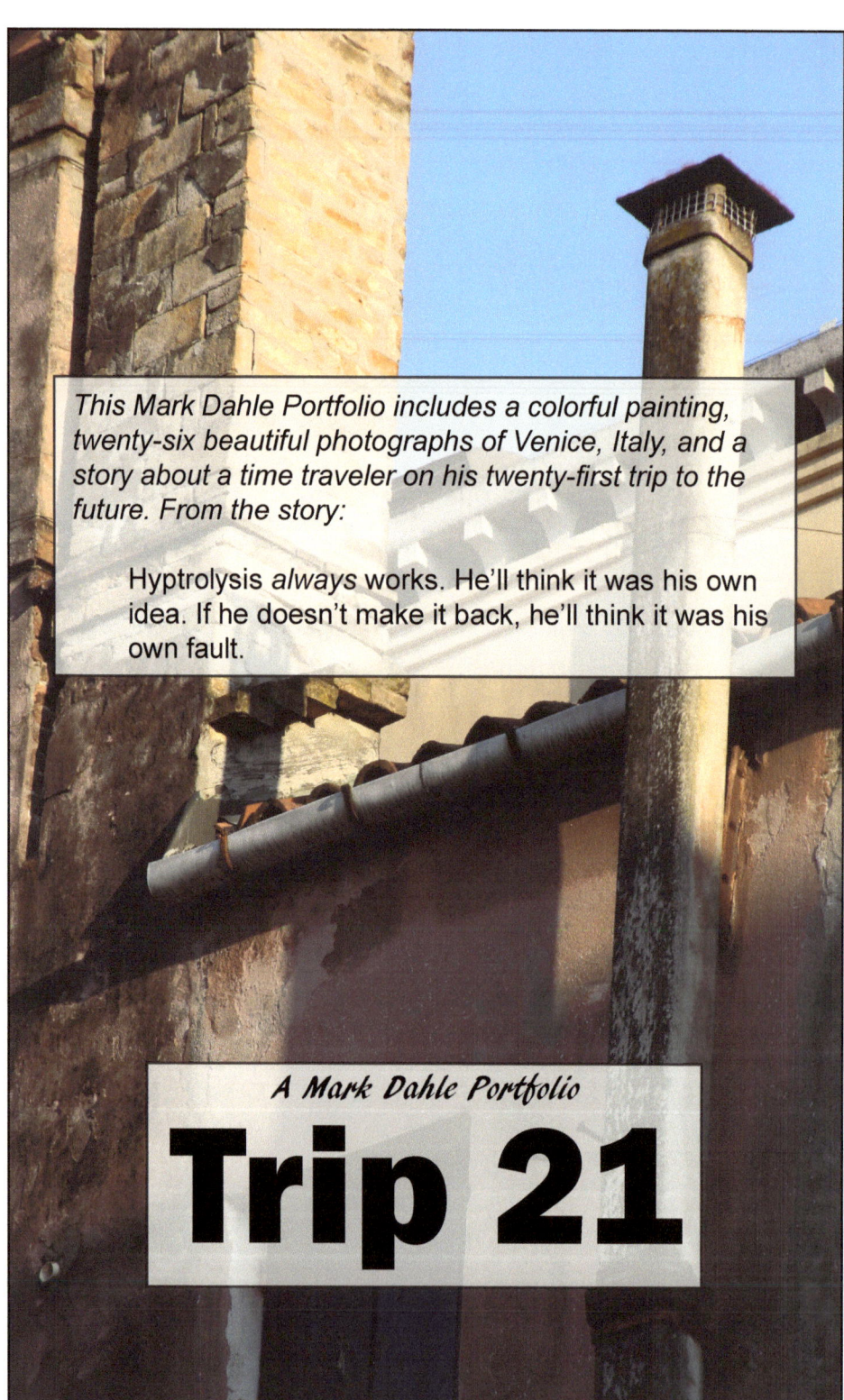

This Mark Dahle Portfolio includes a colorful painting, twenty-six beautiful photographs of Venice, Italy, and a story about a time traveler on his twenty-first trip to the future. From the story:

Hyptrolysis *always* works. He'll think it was his own idea. If he doesn't make it back, he'll think it was his own fault.

A Mark Dahle Portfolio

Trip 21

This Mark Dahle Portfolio includes a colorful painting, twenty-six beautiful photographs from Detroit, and a story about a carpenter who made fine furniture from scraps.

The carpenter came across the twig one day while scouring the countryside for debris. He had already found a sheet of plastic, a broken piece of plywood and several rusty, bent nails. Those he knew he could use. But the twig? He could not imagine a use for it. Nevertheless, it caught his attention as he walked along the edge of a forest. He absentmindedly picked it up.

A Mark Dahle Portfolio

The Carpenter And The Twig

A Mark Dahle Portfolio

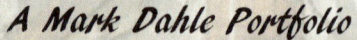

Amanda Gets A Pumpkin

(#1 in the series "Amanda Wanted A Miracle")

This Mark Dahle Portfolio includes a colorful painting, twenty-four beautiful industrial photographs from Beijing, Shangahi and Xian, and a story about a girl who wanted a miracle.

"Oh dear," said her grandmother. "You didn't want a pumpkin? Perhaps we'll have to try again."

www.ingramcontent.com/pod-product-compliance
Lightning Source LLC
Chambersburg PA
CBHW040918180526
45159CB00002BA/523